Withdrawn

Genetics:
UNLOCKING THE SECRETS OF LIFE

Essential Library

An Imprint of Abdo Publishing | www.abdopublishing.com

History of
Science

Genetics:
UNLOCKING THE
SECRETS OF LIFE

by Jillian Lokere

Content Consultant

Mark Borrello
Associate Professor
Program in the History of Science, Technology, and Medicine
University of Minnesota

History of
Science

www.abdopublishing.com

Published by Abdo Publishing, a division of ABDO, PO Box 398166, Minneapolis, Minnesota 55439. Copyright © 2015 by Abdo Consulting Group, Inc. International copyrights reserved in all countries. No part of this book may be reproduced in any form without written permission from the publisher. Essential Library™ is a trademark and logo of Abdo Publishing.

Printed in the United States of America, North Mankato, Minnesota

102014
012015

Cover Photos: Shutterstock Images; Thinkstock
Interior Photos: Shutterstock Images, 1, 3, 11, 48, 65; Thinkstock, 1, 3; Michael Reynolds/epa/Corbis, 7; Patrick Landmann/Science Source, 8; Leslie E. Kossoff/AP Images, 14; Bettmann/Corbis, 19, 76; Field Museum Library/Getty Images, 21; Red Line Editorial, 23, 43; Vit Simanek/CTK Photo/AP Images, 25; iStockphoto, 29, 33; Lester V. Bergman/Corbis, 31; SPL/Science Source, 35, 61; Alila Medical Media/Shutterstock Images, 37; Ned M. Seidler/National Geographic Society/Corbis, 39; David Scharf/Corbis, 41; Francis Leroy, Biocosmos/Science Source, 46; Ellis Bosworth/AP Images, 51; Science Source, 54, 52, 57, 59; A. Barrington Brown/Science Source, 63; Salk Institute/AP Images, 67; Jacopin/BSIP/SuperStock, 70; Andrea Danti/Shutterstock Images, 73; Penni Gladstone/San Francisco Chronicle/Corbis, 83; National Institutes of Health, 75; Sea Wave/Shutterstock Images, 80; Sergey Nivens/Shutterstock Images, 85; Paul Clements/AP Images, 87; Michael Kooren/Reuters/Corbis, 91; Tim Johnson/AP Images, 94; Advanced Cell Technologies/AP Images, 89; Paul Sakuma/AP Images, 92; 454 Life Sciences/PR NewsFoto/AP Images, 97

Editor: Arnold Ringstad
Series Designer: Craig Hinton

Library of Congress Control Number: 2014943852

Cataloging-in-Publication Data
Lokere, Jillian.
 Genetics: unlocking the secrets of life / Jillian Lokere.
  p. cm. -- (History of science)
ISBN 978-1-62403-562-3 (lib. bdg.)
Includes bibliographical references and index.
1. Genetics--History--Juvenile literature. 2. DNA--Juvenile literature. I. Title.
576.5--dc23

2014943852

Contents

The Human
GENOME PROJECT

On June 26, 2000, President Bill Clinton stood before a crowd of reporters at the White House. The day's briefing would not be about a political or military situation. Instead, it would be about one of the most exciting scientific breakthroughs in human history. Two men representing rival scientific groups flanked him. Francis Collins and J. Craig Venter each led a separate effort to decode the human genome, the set of instructions inside human cells that makes it possible for the body to function, grow, and reproduce. For the first time, scientists would be able to read the entirety of the human genetic code. Now, they were joining together to celebrate milestones toward the completion of this goal. Collins's effort was known as the Human Genome Project. Venter worked as head of his own company, Celera Genomics.

A museum exhibit features a figure of a person covered in letters representing the human genome.

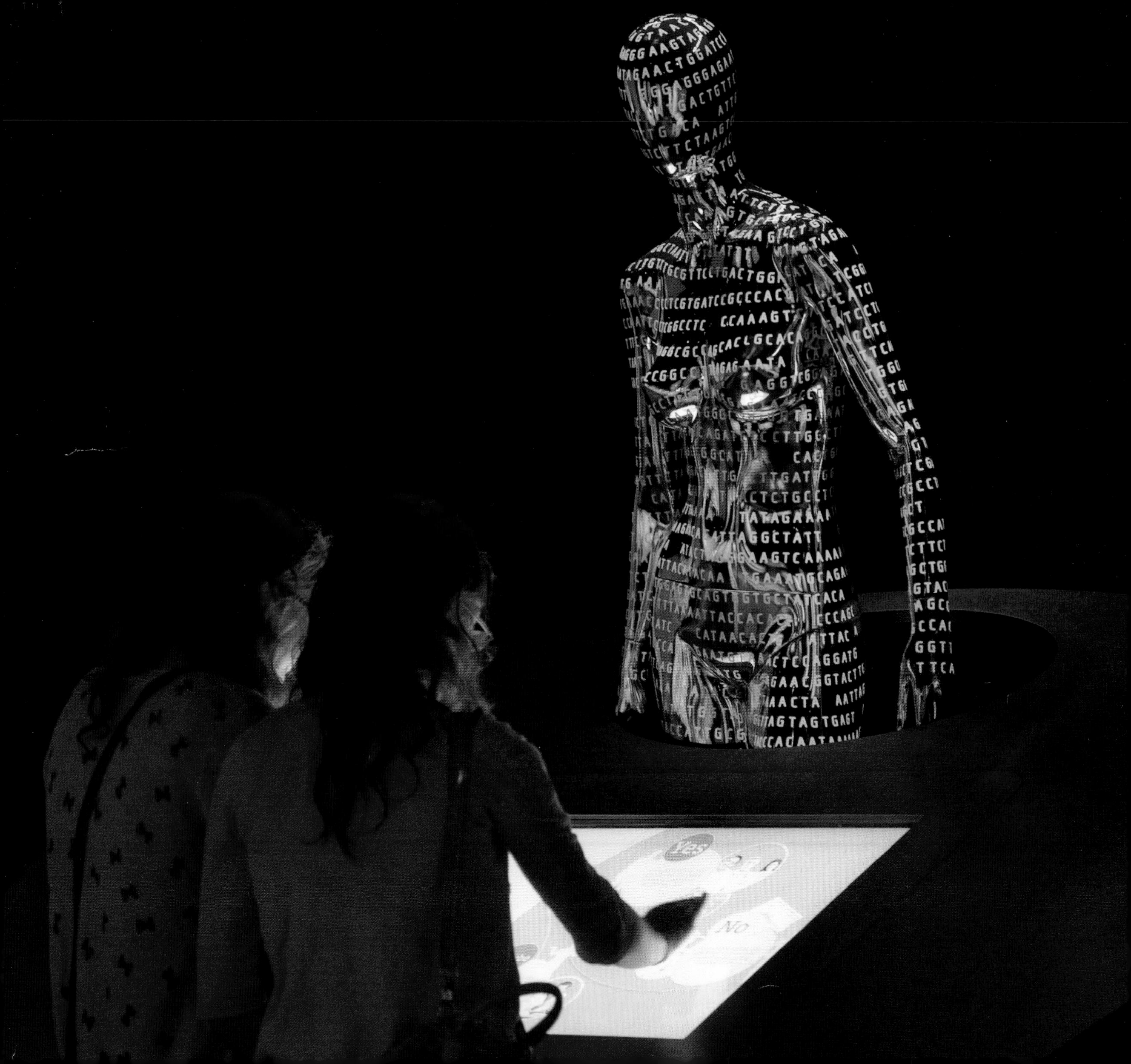
Yes
No

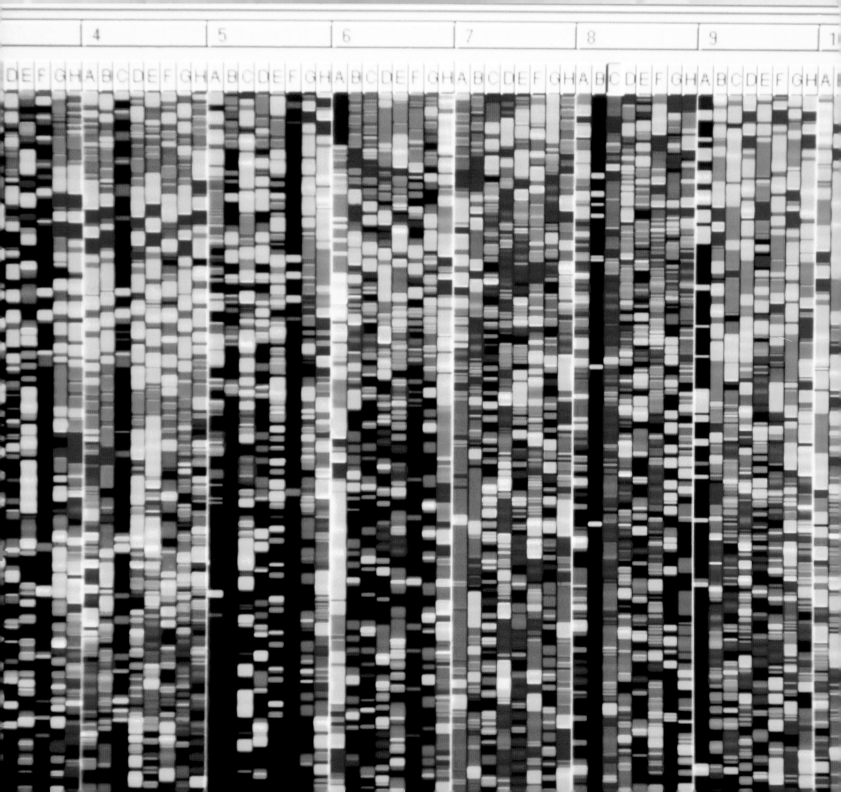

Clinton announced, "We are here to celebrate the completion of the first survey of the entire human genome. Without a doubt, this is the most important, most wondrous map ever produced by humankind. . . . More than 1,000 researchers across six nations have revealed nearly all 3 billion letters of our miraculous genetic code. I congratulate all of you on this stunning and humbling achievement."[1] Collins and Venter then took the stage to discuss the significance of the announcement. They also downplayed their rivalry. Collins said, "The only race we're interested in today is the human race."[2]

In the years since the June 2000 press conference, Venter, Collins, and other scientists have made many more breakthroughs in the field of genetics. A more complete version of the human genome was announced in April 2003. Researchers continue refining and analyzing the genome to this day.

Heredity

Why does a child look like one biological parent but not the other? Why do certain diseases seem to run in the family? These questions have to do with heredity. Heredity is the passage of traits from parents to their offspring. A little more than a century ago, scientists discovered we inherit these traits through genes carried on chromosomes within our cells. Genes, the basic units of heredity, are made up of deoxyribonucleic acid (DNA). DNA molecules are long strands composed of smaller molecules called nucleotide bases. There are four possible bases in these sequences.

Computer technology has made it simple to quickly visualize and analyze human genes.

THE SECRET CODE OF LIFE

Chromosomes are found in the nuclei of cells. Each chromosome consists of a tightly wound piece of DNA. DNA's four nucleotide bases are called adenine, thymine, guanine, and cytosine. The nucleotides are joined into pairs, forming the rungs of a helical, ladder-shaped structure. Adenine only pairs with thymine, and guanine only pairs with cytosine. All genes are made up of sequences of these nucleotides, arranged in different orders and in different lengths. Specialized parts within a cell can read the code and translate it into instructions on how to assemble proteins. RNA helps to transport the instructions. Other parts then assemble the proteins according to the code. Once the proteins are made, cells use them to carry out the functions of life.

The bases' order makes up the genetic code. Cells are able to interpret this code as instructions. Different sets of code are orders to create different proteins, the basic molecules that make up our bodies' structures. Another molecule, called ribonucleic acid (RNA), helps facilitate the creation of these proteins from the genetic instructions.

Once scientists discovered these facts in the 1900s, it became clear that reading the human genetic code could lead to exciting new developments in science and medicine. But the task seemed impossibly daunting. The complete set of human genes contains more than 3 billion bases.[3] One person typing on a keyboard for eight hours per day would take more than 50 years to complete the genome. Yet human cells copy the entire sequence in a matter of hours when they reproduce.[4] Mapping out an entire human genome represented an enormous technical challenge. Still, scientists pressed onward. A formal project to map the genome began in the 1980s. In the ensuing decades, researchers developed new and faster ways to read the genome. Finally, a completed first draft of the sequence was revealed in the year 2000.

DNA and RNA both consist of long series of nucleotide bases.

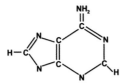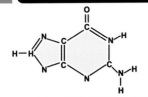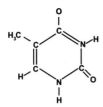
ATCG's   AUCG's

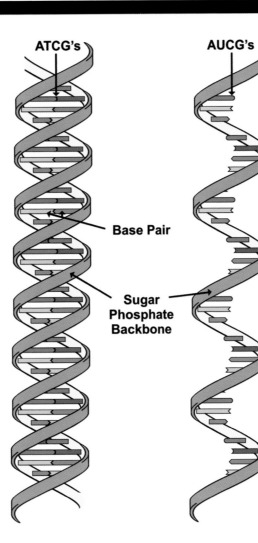

Base Pair

Sugar Phosphate Backbone

DNA
Deoxyribonucleic Acid

RNA
Ribonucleic Acid

Cytosine

Guanine
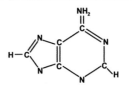

Adenine
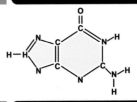

Uracil

Replaces Thymine in RNA

Nucleotide Bases

A Big Project

In 1985, Robert Sinsheimer, the chancellor of the University of California, Santa Cruz, thought a major project might bring more publicity to his university. He decided that reading through the entire sequence of the human genome, a process known as sequencing, would be a suitable project. Sinsheimer gathered a group of scientists to discuss the idea. One year later, Salk Institute cancer researcher Renato Dulbecco published a well-read paper about cancer. He wrote, "We are at a turning point. . . . Research on cancer would receive a major boost from the detailed knowledge of DNA."[5] That same year, the US Department of Energy's Charles DeLisi and Alvin Trivelpiece proposed sequencing the human genome to support a project to detect radiation-induced mutations. This project had been an interest of that agency since the US dropped radiation-emitting atomic bombs on the Japanese cities of Hiroshima and Nagasaki during World War II (1939–1945). The growing buzz about a major human genome sequencing project was met with support from many scientists.

In 1988, Congress awarded the Department of Energy $10.7 million and the National Institutes of Health $17.2 million to launch the Human Genome Project.[6] The project officially began on October 1, 1990, with a planned completion date of 2005. No one group was responsible for the huge project. Instead, there was widespread cooperation among dozens of research centers located in the United States, the United Kingdom, Europe, China, and Japan.

At its beginning, the total cost of the project was estimated at $3 billion.[7] This figure came from multiplying the average sequencing cost of $1 per nucleotide base by the estimated 3 billion bases in the human genome. Although $3 billion is a large sum of money, it is relatively small compared with some other major scientific endeavors, such as the International Space Station.

The Human Genome Project was so large that researchers decided to break the project down into smaller goals. Some participants worked to improve gene sequencing technology. Others developed databases to store sequence information. Researchers created better computer algorithms to analyze the sequencing data. The completion of the Human Genome Project relied on the development of technology that did not exist when the project was first planned. In 1985, scientists in a laboratory could sequence only 500 bases per day by hand. At this rate, sequencing the full genome would have taken more than 16,000 years.[8]

SCIENTIFIC MEGAPROJECTS

The original estimated cost of the Human Genome Project was $3 billion. It actually ended up costing $2.7 billion.[9] By comparison, some other major scientific projects were much more expensive.

Project Apollo, the program to send US astronauts to the moon, took place during the 1960s and 1970s. It cost approximately $20 billion at the time. This adds up to approximately $110 billion in today's dollars.[10] The International Space Station, an orbiting research laboratory built and operated by a group of national space programs, cost approximately $100 billion by 2010.[11] Even earthbound scientific projects have been more expensive. The Large Hadron Collider, a machine that smashes subatomic particles together, was constructed underground near Geneva, Switzerland. It cost approximately $4.75 billion to build.[12]

Unexpected Competition

The Human Genome Project team worked steadily. Still, by 1997, only 3 percent of the genome had been sequenced, even though more than $1.8 billion had been spent.[13] Although sequencing technology had improved since 1985, it was still too slow. Many scientists and political leaders began to doubt that the target date of 2005 could be met. Then came an announcement by J. Craig Venter. In May 1998, Venter announced he would partner with Applied Biosystems, a company that manufactured automated DNA sequencing machines, to form Celera Genomics. Venter promised Celera would sequence the entire human genome in just three years at a fraction of the cost of the publicly funded project.

How was this to be accomplished? In the publicly funded project, DNA was broken into large chunks whose positions on the chromosome were known already. The chunks were further broken into small fragments, and each fragment was sequenced. A computer then analyzed these short sequences. It searched for areas where fragments overlapped and then assembled them into a single long sequence. There were always some gaps, so a slow, painstaking process of resequencing certain areas was used to fill the gaps. As a result, the project proceeded slowly, chunk by chunk.

Venter had a new idea, known as shotgun sequencing. In his plan, the entire human genome was shredded into small fragments. Fast, automated machines

Celera Genomics's DNA sequencing machines made it possible to decode the genome more quickly than before.

sequenced as much of each fragment as was possible. Some fragments were only partially sequenced. All of the sequence data was fed into a supercomputer and assembled. There were many gaps, but Venter did not worry about them, focusing instead on completing a rough draft of the genome.

With Venter's announcement, the race was on. In response, Francis Collins, head of the publicly funded project, decided to speed up his team's efforts. Collins largely abandoned the slower process in favor of Celera's rough-draft model. Teams on both sides worked around the clock.

Reading Humanity

On June 26, 2000, President Clinton announced the completion of rough drafts of the entire human genome by both the public project and Celera Genomics. Data from the public project was published in the journal *Nature* on February 15, 2001. Celera Genomics published its data in the journal *Science* on February 16, 2001. Celera then abandoned further work to refine the genome, instead pursuing projects the company felt would be more profitable. The public project continued filling in gaps and fixing errors. The announcement of the essentially complete genome sequence was made in early 2003. In May 2006, the finished sequence of the last human chromosome was published in *Nature*.

The completion of the Human Genome Project marked a turning point in human history. However, the incredible accomplishment did not come out of nowhere. An enormous amount of work over the preceding century led to humanity's understanding of its own genome. Just a few hundred years ago, no one understood that heredity information comes from both parents. No one understood why or how certain traits could be passed on. Through incredible effort and diligent study, a chain of scientists solved the amazing puzzle that is the genetic code.

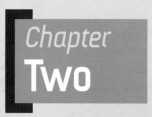

A Gardener
DISCOVERS GENES

Great thinkers had been asking questions about heredity for thousands of years. However, very little progress was made in this field until the 1800s. And when progress did come, very few people took any notice of it at first.

The modern science of genetics began with gardening. Gregor Mendel seemed very unlikely to make major scientific breakthroughs. He had long dreamed of becoming a teacher, but he lacked the funds to attend a university, so he instead became a monk. Mendel lived at a monastery in Brünn, in what is now part of the Czech Republic. The abbot of his monastery recognized Mendel's talent for science and sent him to the University of Vienna in Austria. There Mendel thrived, taking classes in mathematics, physics, statistics, chemistry, and botany. He graduated in 1853 and returned to the monastery.

The father of modern genetics, Gregor Mendel, conducted his pioneering research using pea plants.

Mendel then made a simple request with far-reaching consequences. He had observed that the common pea plants in the monastery garden had various traits. He was interested in understanding how these traits passed from parent plants to their offspring. In 1854, he asked for permission to use a plot of the monastery garden for scientific study. The request was granted.

Mendel Prepares His Experiments

For his experiments in how traits are passed to offspring, Mendel selected seven traits to track. The position of the flower was either axial, along the stem, or terminal, at the tip of the stem. Its color could be purple or white. The plant's height was either tall or short. The shape of the peas could be round or wrinkled, and the peas' color was either yellow or green. Finally, the pea pod could appear inflated or constricted, and its color was either yellow or green.

Before beginning his experiments, Mendel spent two years making sure his plants had consistent, controlled traits. He bred them so that plants with a certain form of

Mendel chose traits that would be easy to distinguish in pea plants.

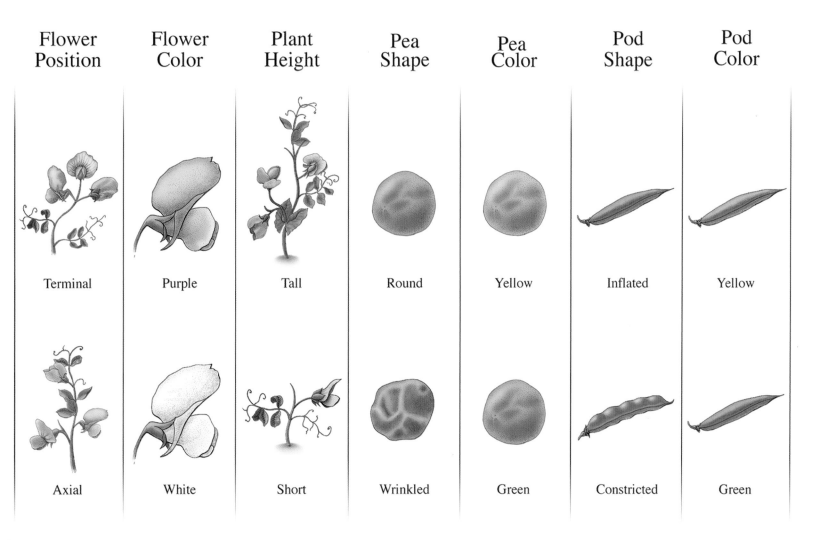

Flower Position	Flower Color	Plant Height	Pea Shape	Pea Color	Pod Shape	Pod Color
Terminal	Purple	Tall	Round	Yellow	Inflated	Yellow
Axial	White	Short	Wrinkled	Green	Constricted	Green

a trait always had offspring plants with that same form all of the time. In 1856, he was ready to start experiments in crossbreeding.

Mendel's Experiments

Mendel's first experiment crossed parent plants that differed in only one trait, such as seed color. Mendel bred a plant having yellow seeds with a plant having green seeds. In the first generation of offspring, called F1, all of the plants had yellow seeds. None of the offspring had green seeds. Seeing this result, Mendel designated yellow as the dominant form of the seed color trait. He called green the recessive form of the trait. Other traits showed similar results, with one form showing up in all of the offspring.

Mendel next wanted to see if the recessive forms of the traits would reappear in later generations. He allowed all of the F1 plants to self-fertilize, meaning egg cells and pollen cells from the same plant were crossed. Most of the resulting plants, called the F2 generation, had yellow seeds. However, a few had green seeds. Mendel then counted how many plants showed each form of the trait. He found the

COUNTING IS KEY

Mendel repeated his crosses with all seven trait categories and carefully counted the resulting offspring. Mendel's devotion to counting and statistics may have been influenced by his mathematical studies at the University of Vienna. Counting the ratios of the traits proved to be critical to understanding heredity. Previous naturalists had obtained similar results to those of Mendel. However, they had failed to count the numbers of offspring of each kind, preventing them from seeing the ratios and patterns that hinted at the true nature of genetics.

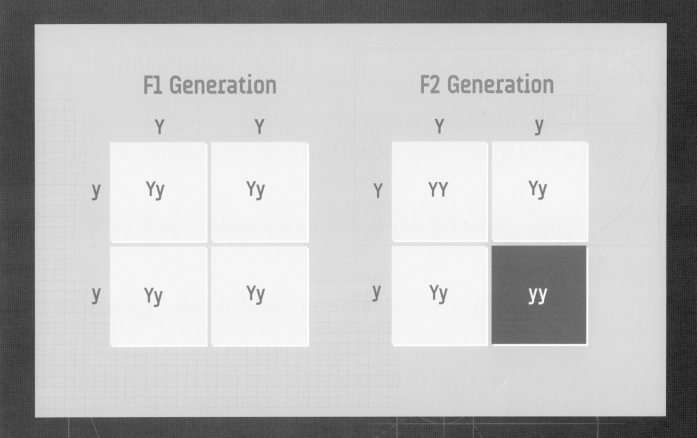

PUNNETT SQUARES

Punnett squares are tools used to see the possible genetics of offspring from a given set of parents. They combine the parent's alleles for a trait and show the ratio of sets of alleles in the offspring. In the above example, *Y* is the dominant allele for yellow seed color, and *y* is the recessive allele for green seed color. The parents of the F1 generation are purebred; one parent has two dominant Y alleles and the other has two recessive y alleles. All of the offspring have Yy alleles for the seed color trait. As a result, they all have yellow seeds. These became the parents of the F2 generation. One fourth of the F2 generation had YY alleles and one half had Yy alleles. These all have yellow seeds. One fourth of the F2 generation had yy alleles, giving them green seeds.

ratio was almost exactly 3:1. There were approximately three yellow-seeded plants for each green-seeded plant. Mendel repeated these experiments many times with all seven of the traits he had identified. He continued to find the same 3:1 ratio in the F2 generation.

Discovering Genes

Based on these results, Mendel hypothesized the existence of genes, physical parts inside plants that resulted in heredity. A gene, Mendel thought, could come in one of two forms, later called alleles. Each reproductive cell, or germ cell, from a parent must contain two alleles for each trait. Each allele can be either dominant or recessive. When the parent cells combine, the resulting offspring will randomly inherit one allele from each parent. Mendel reasoned that when he crossed yellow-seeded plants with green-seeded plants, the F1 generation must have had one yellow allele and one green allele. Because the yellow allele is dominant over the green allele, the entire generation had yellow seeds. The F1 generation had the green seed allele, but because it was recessive, it remained hidden. This was proven in the F2 generation, when the green seed color reappeared in one-third of the offspring.

To further support his hypothesis, Mendel continued studying the yellow-seeded F2 plants. He allowed them to self-fertilize. He found that one-third of the F2 plants produced all yellow-seeded offspring. Mendel concluded those plants had two copies of the yellow seed color allele. The only way for the recessive trait to occur

Mendel's manuscripts sit in museums today, but they were largely ignored when originally published.

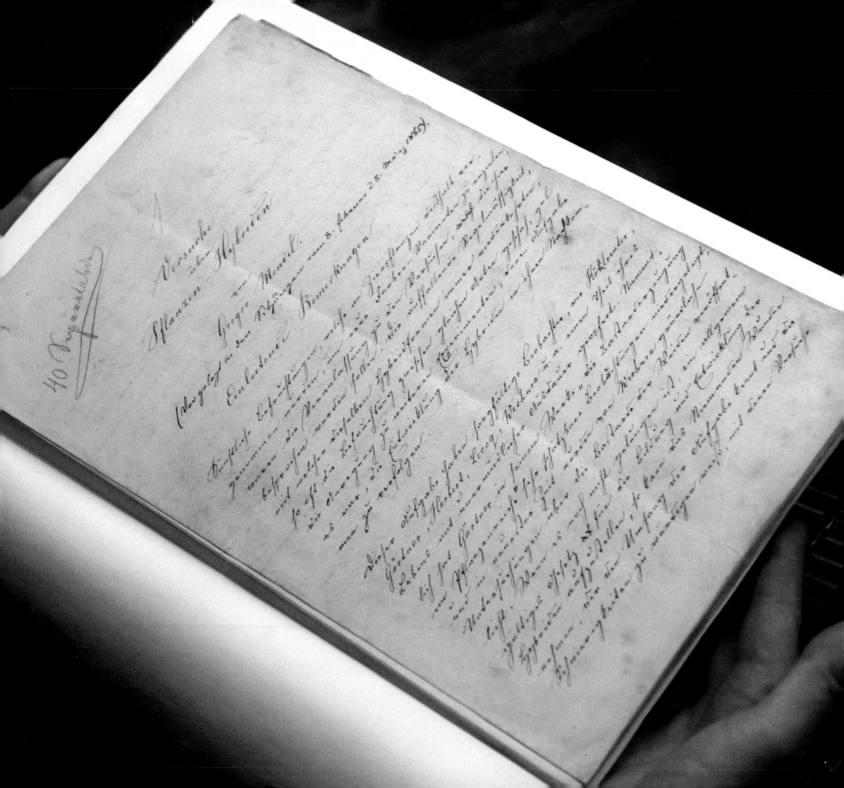

Versuche
über
Pflanzen-Hybriden

von Gregor Mendel.

(Vorgelegt in den Sitzungen vom 8. Februar 28. März 1865).

Einleitende Bemerkungen

MENDEL'S LAWS

Mendel's conclusions can be summed up in the following laws:

1. **The Law of Segregation:** Each inherited trait is defined by a gene pair. Parent genes are randomly separated to the parent's germ cells. Each germ cell contains only one gene of the pair. When the parents' germ cells come together, the offspring inherits one gene from each parent.

2. **The Law of Independent Assortment:** Genes for different traits are sorted separately from one another. The inheritance of one trait is not dependent on the inheritance of another.

3. **The Law of Dominance:** An organism with more than one form of a gene will show the form that is dominant.

was for the plant to have both of its seed color alleles be the recessive ones. The other F2 plants produced yellow-seeded and green-seeded offspring in the now-familiar 3:1 ratio. He concluded these plants must have had one copy of the yellow allele and one copy of the green allele.

Mendel next continued with precise experiments following two traits at a time, such as seed color and seed shape. He was able to show that each of the seven traits he studied was inherited independently. In other words, the trait for seed color is passed on in a way that does not depend on the trait for seed shape.

Unfortunately for Mendel, his work was not appreciated in his lifetime. In 1865, more than a decade after he began his studies, he presented his findings to leading scientists of the day. A year later, he published his findings and distributed copies of his work. But his lack of traditional scientific credentials meant he was completely ignored. It would be more than 30 years before the scientific community caught up.

What Mendel discovered would eventually revolutionize the study of heredity. His findings would come to be known as Mendel's laws. Although we know now that heredity is more complex than this simple set of rules, Mendel's ideas still form the basis of the modern understanding of genetics.

Mendel's experiments and conclusions were elegant and accurate. However, the scientific world of the 1860s was not ready to appreciate them. Mendel died in 1884, unrecognized for his discoveries.

Chapter Three

Making Sense OF MENDEL

A new field of study called cell biology was on the rise in Europe in the 1840s. Two scientists, Theodor Schwann and Matthias J. Schleiden, began using improved microscopes to study cells, theorizing that these tiny objects inside living things are the fundamental building blocks of life. Their theory became known as the Schleiden-Schwann cell theory.

Their microscopes allowed Schleiden and Schwann to see more clearly than ever before into the inner workings of cells. They could see the nucleus, the cellular structure now known to contain the cell's chromosomes. Even though Schleiden and Schwann did not understand fully what the nucleus does, they noticed it seemed to play a role in cell division.

The explanation for Mendel's results lay within cells, the building blocks that make up all life.

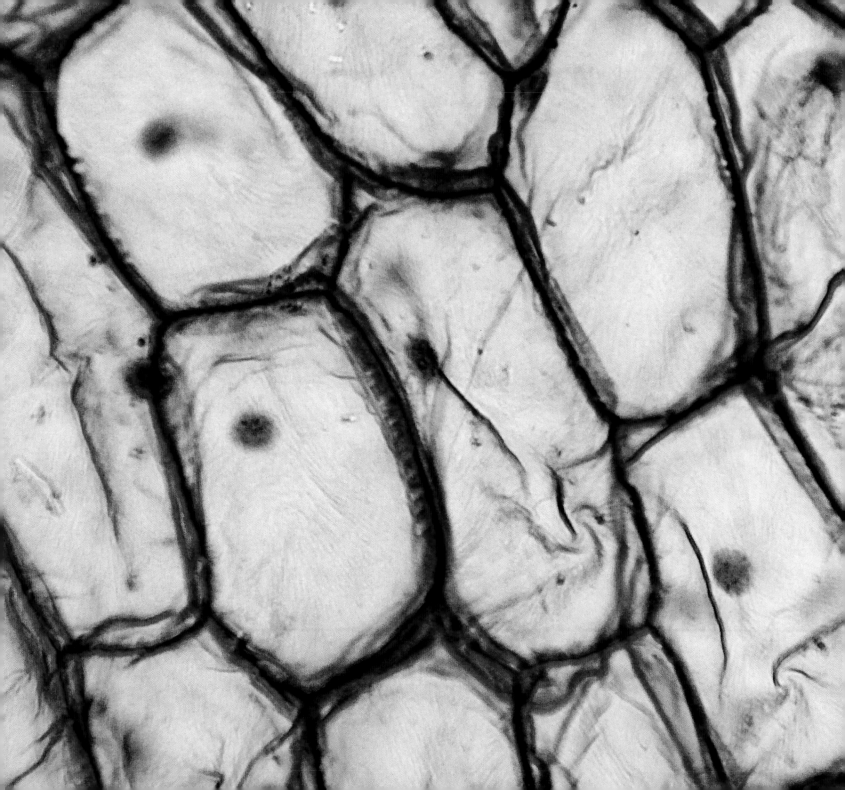

THE WRONG PATH OF INHERITANCE

English scientist Charles Darwin is famous for his book *On the Origin of Species*, which in 1859 put forward the theory of evolution by natural selection. Because Darwin was a well-respected naturalist, his findings were taken seriously. In a book about heredity in 1868, Darwin suggested offspring could inherit traits they acquired. This idea is often called Lamarckism, after French scientist Jean-Baptiste Lamarck, who had presented his theory of acquired characteristics in the early 1800s. Later experiments, in which scientists cut the tails off mice, proved this idea wrong when all of the mice's offspring had tails. But at the time, Darwin's idea was taken seriously. Unlike his theory of evolution, his ideas about heredity were nearly all wrong. Still, scientists of the day ignored or were unaware of Mendel's better-supported findings.

In 1851, Robert Remak built on the Schleiden-Schwann cell theory. He showed that cell division was the method by which cells reproduced. In 1874, Remak's student, Leopold Auerbach, published a series of drawings of the large, clear germ cells of a species of threadworm. In the drawings, the fusing of two nuclei can be seen. Another scientist, Oscar Hertwig, was studying sea urchin germ cells around the same time. He noticed that a few minutes after sperm cells were added to a dish containing egg cells, a second nucleus appeared in many of the eggs. He put forward the revolutionary theory that the egg and sperm nuclei fused during fertilization.

In 1879, Walther Flemming used a dye to stain cells during cell division. He saw strands of a substance within the nucleus of cells that he called chromatin. He showed that the threads shortened and thickened during cell division. Flemming called the structures made of these threads chromosomes. During cell division, the chromosomes split lengthwise into two halves, and the halves moved to opposite sides of the cell. He called this process mitosis.

During the process of mitosis, chromosomes copy themselves, giving each new cell a complete set of identical genes.

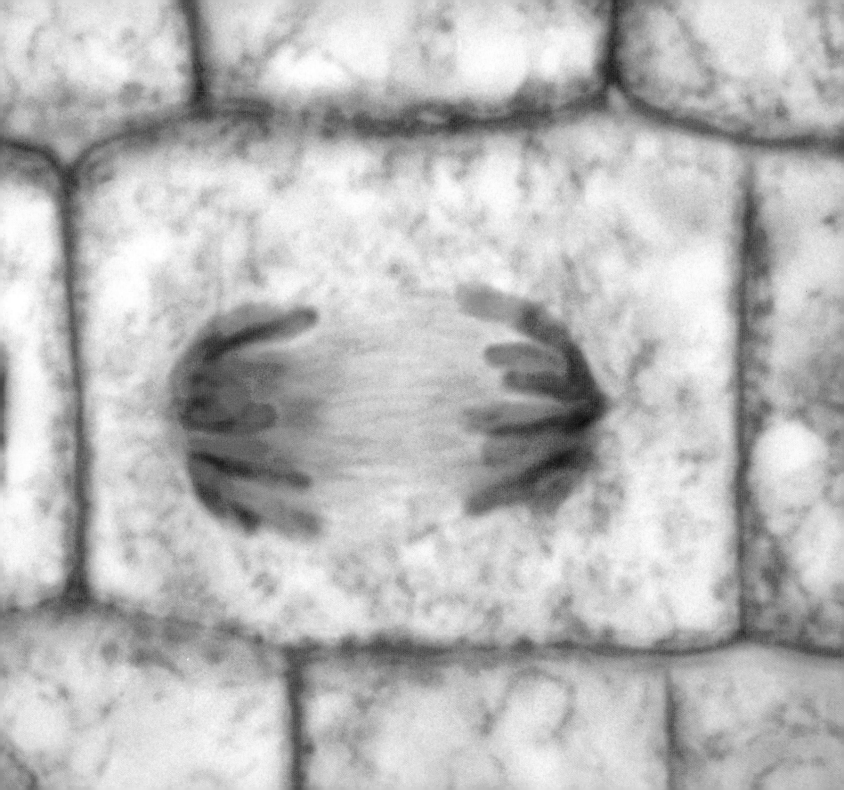

In the 1870s, German cell biologists established a station for studying marine organisms near Naples, Italy. They looked locally for organisms to study and noticed sea urchin eggs. Under the microscope, the urchin cells were so transparent the scientists could easily see what was happening inside them. When Hertwig was developing his theory of fertilization, he could see the nucleus of the sperm as a dark circle against the lighter background of the egg cell. The sperm nucleus grew when it entered the egg, and it moved toward the egg's nucleus. He watched as the two small circles met and slowly became one.

The nongerm cells of organisms' bodies constantly undergo mitosis to replace dead cells.

Another key discovery came in 1891. German biochemist Albrecht Kossel announced he had successfully isolated guanine and adenine, two of the nucleotide bases found in DNA. Two years later he isolated the other two bases, thymine and cytosine. It would be several decades before scientists grasped the importance of these bases in heredity.

Rediscovering Mendel's Work

Around the year 1900, three scientists independently replicated Mendel's published work: Hugo de Vries, Erich von Tschermak, and Carl Correns. De Vries was a professor of botany at the University of Amsterdam in the Netherlands. Von Tschermak was a scientist at the Halle-Wittenberg University in Germany. Correns was a tutor at the University of Tübingen in Germany. The three scientists rediscovered Mendel's laws of inheritance from their own plant experiments.

Sea urchins proved to be extremely useful in the early history of cell biology.

Mendel's results were finally entering widespread acceptance. But there remained another key discovery to be made. Scientists worked to learn the connection between heredity and chromosomes.

Heredity and Chromosomes

German biologist Theodor Boveri made the next key breakthrough. Using sea urchin eggs, Boveri demonstrated a particular number of chromosomes was required for the urchins' normal development. He realized in 1902 that this meant each individual chromosome must have a specific function. Boveri suggested chromosomes might be responsible for heredity.

At approximately the same time in Kansas, Walter Sutton, a young graduate student, was studying spermatocytes, the cells that give rise to sperm cells. He studied these cells in grasshoppers. Sutton saw that spermatocytes paired up their chromosomes and created a copy of each pair. This left each cell with four complete copies of each chromosome instead of the normal two copies seen in somatic cells, the nongerm cells that make up the bodies of organisms. The spermatocyte then divided, resulting in two daughter cells that each had two copies of the chromosomes. Finally, the daughter cells divided again. The final result was four cells, each with one copy of each chromosome. These four cells were the sperm cells. Sutton called this cell division process meiosis. Unlike mitosis, meiosis was only used to create germ cells.

Boveri's hypothesis about chromosomes' role in heredity was proven several years after he suggested it.

Mitosis

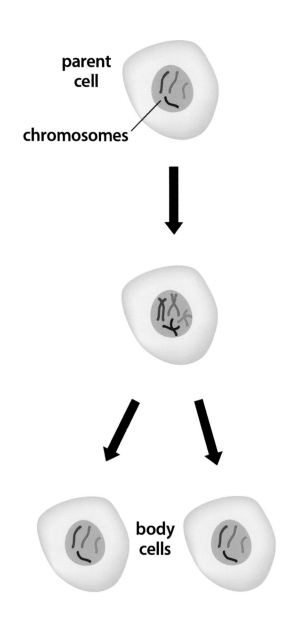

parent cell

chromosomes

body cells

Meiosis

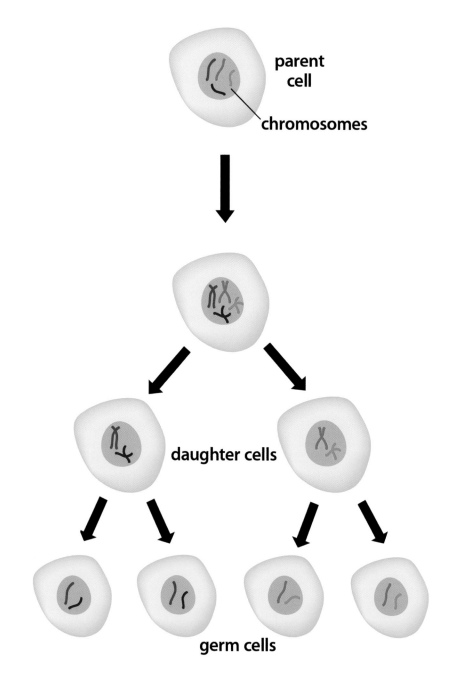

parent cell

chromosomes

daughter cells

germ cells

Like Boveri, Sutton published his work in 1902. He wrote that it was logical for genes to be on chromosomes. The final result of meiosis, germ cells with one copy of each chromosome, fit with Mendel's theories. Combining two germ cells to create a new organism would give the organism a pair of chromosomes. Then, the new organism's traits would be determined by whether it had dominant or recessive genes on the two chromosomes.

Sutton realized each chromosome must carry more than one gene. Otherwise there could only be as many traits in an organism as there were chromosomes, which is clearly false. Together, the conclusions of Sutton and Boveri came to be called the Sutton-Boveri chromosome theory of inheritance.

However, Sutton introduced one new idea. He suggested some traits on the same chromosome might be inherited together. This idea of linked genes was explored in depth over the next decade. The key to this research would be the humble fruit fly.

Mitosis is used to create new body cells, while meiosis is used to create new germ cells.

Mapping Genes to CHROMOSOMES

$$\frac{a+b}{a} = \frac{a}{b} = 1{,}618$$

The Sutton-Boveri chromosome theory of inheritance caused a storm of excitement in the scientific world. Some scientists embraced the idea. Others scoffed at it. Among the scoffers was a prominent scientist named Thomas Hunt Morgan. At first he called the idea absurd. However, Morgan later had to admit he was wrong when his own data actually supported the theory.

Sex Determination

In 1891, Morgan was an associate professor of biology at Bryn Mawr College in Pennsylvania. He researched sex determination, the study of how a fertilized egg was influenced to become a male or female animal.

Morgan's work with fruit flies would bring about major advances in the understanding of chromosomes.

His student Nettie Stevens worked with mealworms. She noticed something interesting. During egg cell development, before meiosis, all of the cells contained ten pairs of chromosomes. These matched up perfectly. But this was not the case during sperm cell development. Stevens saw that before meiosis, one of the pairs had one chromosome that was smaller and one that was larger. After meiosis, half of the sperm cells contained the larger member of the pair, and half contained the smaller one.

Stevens carefully kept track of which sperm cells fertilized which eggs. She found that an egg fertilized by the sperm containing the smaller chromosome always went on to become a male mealworm. An egg fertilized by sperm containing the larger chromosome always went on to become a female mealworm. In 1905, she published her results. She argued for what we now call the XY model of sex determination. The chromosomes that determine sex are known as the X and Y chromosomes due to their shape. The X chromosome is much larger than the Y chromosome. An embryo with two X chromosomes becomes a female, while an embryo with one X and one Y becomes a male. The egg always contributes an X, and a sperm can contribute either an X or a Y.

The Fly Room

Although Stevens's data showed the link between chromosomes and sex determination, Morgan was still stubborn. He did not believe the chromosome theory

The tiny fruit fly became a critical organism in the history of genetics.

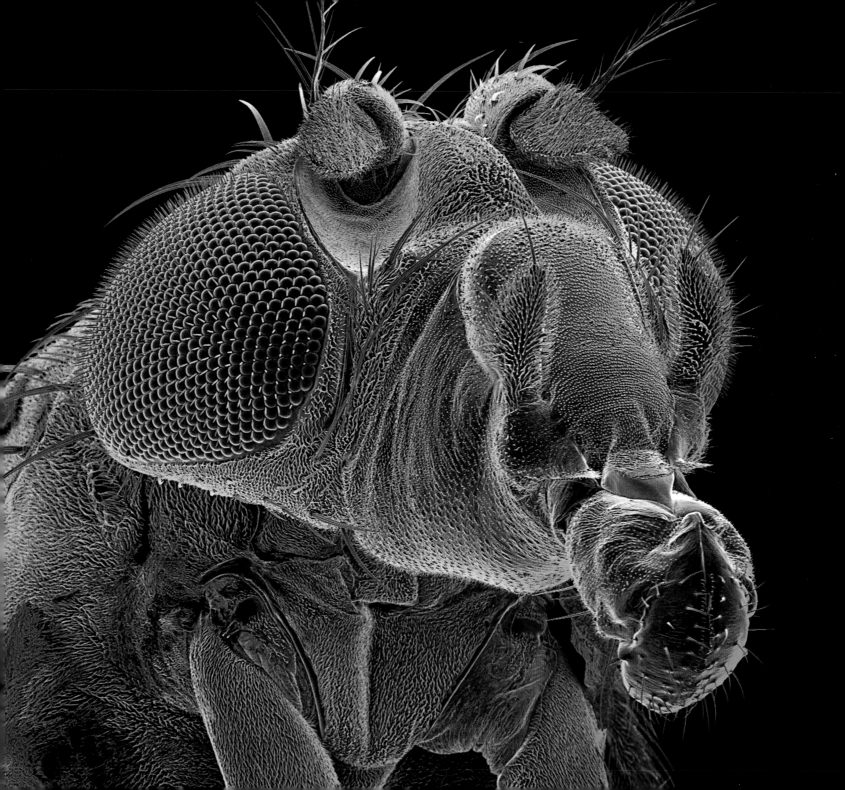

of inheritance or the XY model of sex determination. He moved to Columbia University in New York in 1904. There, he tried to produce new variations in an organism in an effort to create a new species. He settled on the fruit fly, whose scientific name is *Drosophila melanogaster*. Drosophila are small and inexpensive, and they reproduce quickly, making them a good model to study genetics.

In what would become known as his famous "fly room," Morgan exposed fruit flies to various chemicals and X rays in the hopes of producing genetic variations, also called mutations.[1] He and his three students, Calvin Bridges, Hermann Muller, and Alfred Sturtevant, combed through thousands of offspring flies looking for new traits. In June 1910, Morgan noticed one male fruit fly with white eyes instead of the usual red.

Morgan Eats His Words

Morgan mated the white-eyed male fly to an ordinary red-eyed female fly. The resulting offspring in the F1 generation were all red-eyed. He and his students concluded that the white form of the eye color gene must be recessive. When the red-eyed F1 flies were mated together, the offspring had red eyes and white eyes in a 3:1 ratio, just as in Mendel's experiments. However, something else about the flies shocked the scientists. Every one of the white-eyed flies was male.

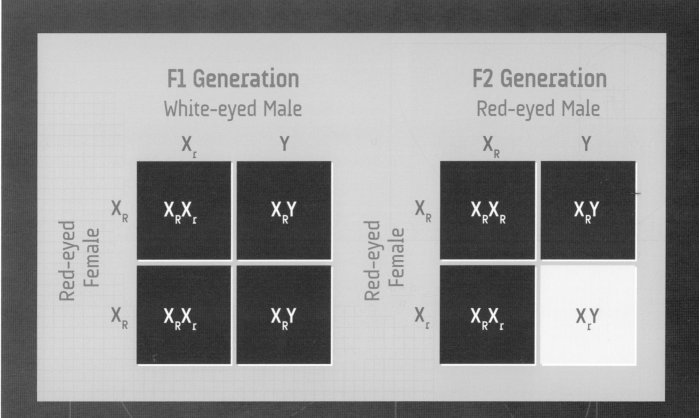

FRUIT FLY PUNNETT SQUARES

These Punnett squares show the F1 and F2 generations produced after breeding a red-eyed female fly to a white-eyed male fly. The results of this experiment helped prove the existence of sex-linked characteristics. The two alleles for the eye color gene are R, the dominant allele that produces red eye color, and r, the recessive allele that produces white eye color. This gene only appears on the X chromosome.

Morgan was astonished. He and his students repeated the crosses but found the same result. He quickly realized that the discovery could be neatly explained by two things: the chromosome theory of inheritance and the XY model of sex determination.

After continuing his work through the early 1910s, Morgan figured out an explanation for his fruit fly results. Males have only one X chromosome. If the gene for eye color were on that chromosome, then a male with white eyes would have just one copy of the mutant allele. A normal red-eyed female would have two copies of the normal red eye color allele, one on each X chromosome. When those flies were crossed, the female F1 offspring would get one X chromosome from the mother and a second from the father. All would have red eyes. The father's X chromosome would have the mutant white-eyed allele. The male F1 offspring would each get an X chromosome from their mother and a Y chromosome from their father. They would only have one allele for eye color, and it would be the mother's red-eyed allele. So, all the males would be red-eyed. When the F1 flies were crossed, the next generation would have a 3:1 ratio of red eyes to white eyes. If a female fly received a white-eyed allele from her father's X chromosome, it would be recessive to her mother's red-eyed allele. However, if a male fly's only X chromosome had the recessive white-eyed allele, it would have white eyes. As a result, all of the white-eyed flies would be male.

Crossing Over

Now convinced of the new ideas, Morgan continued exposing flies to chemicals that would produce mutations, though he did not understand how the mutation process worked. He eventually found a mutant fly with wings only half as long as normal. Just like the white-eyed mutation, the short-winged mutation was linked to the sex-determining X and Y chromosomes. He began mating flies with white eyes and short wings. He managed to breed a female fly that had the white-eye allele on one X chromosome and the short-wing allele on the other. Morgan crossed this fly with a normal male. He expected that half of the resulting sons would have white eyes and normal wings. They would have gotten the mother's X chromosome with the white-eye mutation. He expected the other half of the sons to have red eyes and short wings. They would have gotten the mother's X chromosome with the short-wing mutation. This is mostly what he saw. However, there were a small number of sons with white eyes and short wings. There were also a small number of sons that looked normal.

Again, Morgan was astonished. How could this be? Belgian cytologist Frans Alfons Janssens provided the answer in 1911. He was carefully studying how egg and sperm

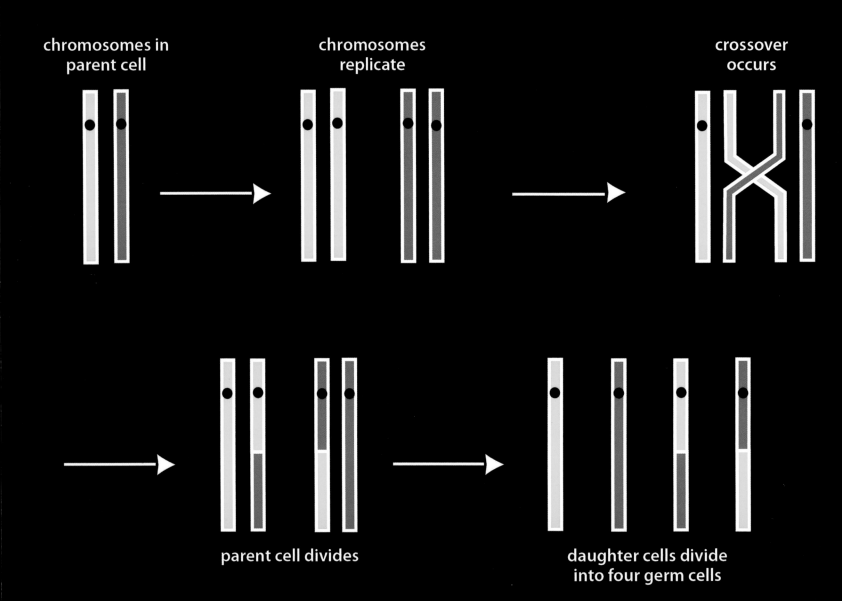

chromosomes in parent cell

chromosomes replicate

crossover occurs

parent cell divides

daughter cells divide into four germ cells

cells formed. He noticed that just after the matching chromosomes began moving apart, they seemed stuck together in certain places. The sticking produced cross-like formations. Janssens theorized that at these sites, the chromosomes exchanged pieces and reconnected. He concluded that fragments of one chromosome could be transferred to another chromosome! The process is now known as crossover. It moves genetic code from one chromosome to the corresponding paired chromosome during meiosis.

Morgan realized his unexpected fly results were connected to Janssens's ideas about crossover. During the development of egg cells, some of the mother's X chromosomes crossed over. This left both mutations, white eyes and short wings, on the same X chromosome. The other X chromosome would be left with normal genes for eye color and wing length. This explained the existence of a few males with white eyes and short wings and a few that looked totally normal.

Going one step further, Morgan hypothesized that genes must have physical locations on chromosomes. He reasoned that the closer together two genes were located on a chromosome, the less likely that crossover could take place between them. Genes farther apart would experience more crossover.

Making a Map of Drosophila Genes

Alfred Henry Sturtevant, the 19-year-old Columbia University undergraduate who was working with Morgan, began the task of mapping out the Drosophila's genes.

The crossover process during meiosis results in four chromosomes with a mix of genes from the organism.

He bred many flies carrying different genetic mutations and looked for crossover in the offspring. In this way, he was able to figure out the locations of the genes on the Drosophila chromosomes.

Chromosome mapping has proved critical to scientists' understanding of our genome. Later, the Human Genome Project would rely on human genetic maps. It helped those scientists assemble the many sequences from DNA fragments into one sequence for an entire human chromosome.

After Morgan's discoveries, scientists understood that genes are located on chromosomes. But they still did not know what genes are actually made of or what they do. How, for example, does a gene make fly eyes red or white? Questions like this would soon be answered using unlikely organisms: bread mold and a bacterium.

Researchers have been breeding and studying fruit flies for more than a century.

Genes, Proteins, AND DNA

$$\frac{a+b}{a} = \frac{a}{b} = 1,618$$

How do genes affect traits? What is it they do to make a fly's eyes white or red? These questions intrigued scientist George W. Beadle. He was a researcher at the California Institute of Technology in the 1930s, where Morgan had moved his lab in 1928. During this time, he studied eye color in fruit flies with Alfred Sturtevant. By 1935 he had found evidence that fly eye color is produced by a series of chemical reactions. However, finding the effect of a single gene mutation on these reactions seemed impossible.

In 1937, Beadle accepted a professorship at Stanford University. Shortly thereafter, he recruited Edward L. Tatum, a scientist skilled at studying cells, to become a research associate in his laboratory. Beadle decided to find a very simple organism to study. He thought a simpler organism might make it easier to figure out the precise

Beadle, pictured at home with his wife, Muriel, later became the president of the University of Chicago.

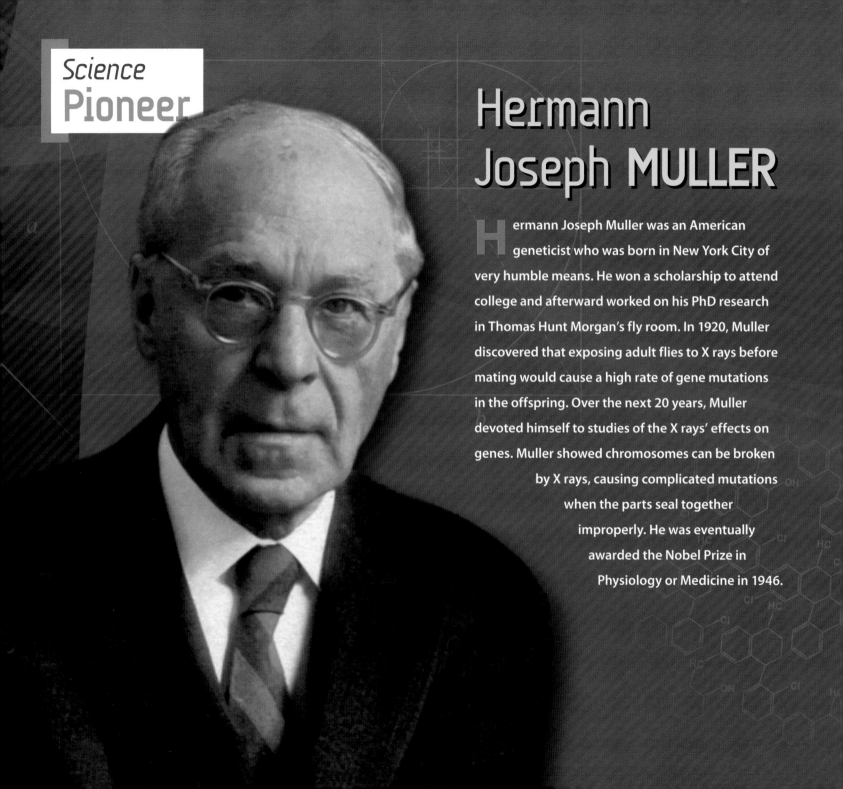

Hermann Joseph MULLER

Hermann Joseph Muller was an American geneticist who was born in New York City of very humble means. He won a scholarship to attend college and afterward worked on his PhD research in Thomas Hunt Morgan's fly room. In 1920, Muller discovered that exposing adult flies to X rays before mating would cause a high rate of gene mutations in the offspring. Over the next 20 years, Muller devoted himself to studies of the X rays' effects on genes. Muller showed chromosomes can be broken by X rays, causing complicated mutations when the parts seal together improperly. He was eventually awarded the Nobel Prize in Physiology or Medicine in 1946.

effects of mutation on cells. He knew that he could use X rays to produce new mutations; this had been demonstrated in the 1920s by Hermann Joseph Muller.

Breakthroughs with Bread Mold

Beadle and Tatum settled on a bread mold called *Neurospora crassa*. Neurospora possesses only one set of seven unpaired chromosomes. Because there is only one copy of each gene, there can be no dominant or recessive alleles. Whichever allele is present on the chromosome will produce the trait, which can then be observed.

Neurospora is grown in a laboratory on a special medium. It can be grown on either a minimal medium or a complete medium. A minimal medium contains some basic nutrients from which the Neurospora can synthesize all it needs to survive and grow. A complete medium contains all the nutrients that Neurospora needs to grow. All the mold needs to do is absorb the nutrients; it does not need to synthesize any nutrients itself.

MULLER'S MUTATIONS

In 1929, Muller gave a lecture to the general public in which he reminisced about his X ray experiments. He said:

All types of mutations, large and small, ugly and beautiful, burst upon the gaze. Flies with bulging eyes or with flat or dented eyes; flies with white, purple, yellow or brown eyes; flies with curly hair, with ruffled hair, with parted hair, with fine and with coarse hair, and bald flies; flies with swollen antennae, or extra antennae, or legs in place of antennae. . . . Big flies and little ones, dark ones and light ones, active and sluggish ones, fertile and sterile ones, long-lived and short-lived ones. . . . The roots of life—the genes—had indeed been struck.[1]

Later in his career, Tatum applied what he had learned from Neurospora to new research on genetics in bacteria.

Beadle and Tatum hypothesized that if a certain mutation removed the ability to synthesize nutrients, the mold would no longer grow on a minimal medium. It would only grow on a complete medium. The duo exposed approximately 5,000 mold specimens to X rays and then put samples of each one on both kinds of medium.[2] In sample number 299, they found what they were looking for.[3] The mold could survive on the complete medium, but died on the minimal medium.

The researchers added back one nutrient at a time to the minimal medium and then tested sample 299 to see if it could grow. They first added single amino acids, the building blocks of protein molecules. None of them allowed sample 299 to grow on the minimal medium. Next the scientists tried vitamins. Finally, when they added a vitamin called biotin to the minimal medium, sample 299 grew.

Beadle and Tatum knew that biotin is generated by a series of chemical reactions that need enzymes made up of protein to function. Therefore, they hypothesized that genes produce protein enzymes. They were later able to prove this with new experiments in which they found three genes required to synthesize the amino acid arginine. They published their findings in 1941. In 1958, they won a joint Nobel Prize in Physiology or Medicine for their work. Their hypothesis became known as the "one gene, one enzyme" model of how genes work. Although later it was refined to include proteins other than enzymes, their hypothesis was a groundbreaking leap forward in understanding the function of genes.

What Are Genes Made Of?

Although scientists were starting to piece together just what genes do in the cell, they still did not know what genes were made of. It was well accepted that genes were

ARE GENES MADE OF PROTEINS?

In 1902, the Sutton-Boveri chromosome theory of inheritance first linked genes with chromosomes. But what part of chromosomes made up the genes? Many scientists in the first part of the 1900s supposed genes were made of proteins because proteins seemed more complex than DNA. Proteins were known to be made up of 20 amino acid building blocks. DNA was known to be made of only four building blocks—the four nucleotide bases adenine, guanine, thymine, and cytosine. Many scientists could not imagine that only four building blocks could create enough complexity to carry genetic information.

located on chromosomes. But which part of chromosomes carried the genetic information? After all, chromosomes are complex biological molecules that contain DNA and many different kinds of proteins.

In 1944, just a few years after Beadle and Tatum published the "one gene, one enzyme" theory, American biologist Oswald Theodore Avery and his colleagues at the Rockefeller Institute in New York performed experiments showing DNA carries genetic information. Avery's team worked with a species of bacteria that causes deadly infections in mice. Not all scientists were convinced of Avery's results, but his experiments were reproduced and confirmed by others. Scientist James Dewey Watson, a researcher at Cambridge University in the United Kingdom, later wrote, "When I arrived at Indiana University in the fall of 1947 with plans to pursue the gene for my PhD thesis, Avery's paper came up over and over in conversations. By then, no one doubted the reproducibility of his results. . . . DNA had at last become an important objective for chemists setting their sights on the next breakthrough."[4] And it

Avery's work proved the DNA molecule played a critical role in heredity and set the stage for the modern science of genetics.

was Watson himself who played a major role in the next major breakthrough: the structure of DNA.

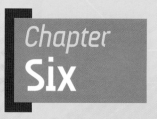

The Double
HELIX

DNA was now understood to be the carrier of genetic information. The race was on to figure out how the molecule accomplished this feat. Watson had a feeling the secret would lie in DNA's structure. During the spring of 1951, Watson attended a conference in which English physicist Maurice Wilkins presented data. Wilkins worked in the laboratory of John T. Randall at King's College London. He studied the three-dimensional structure of biological molecules using X rays. Wilkins's data, obtained with a technique known as X ray diffraction, showed that DNA must have a repeating structure.

Cooperation and Deception

Watson became excited. Finally, answers about DNA's mechanism for storing genetic information seemed to be within reach. He recruited PhD student Francis Harry

X ray diffraction images of DNA revealed repeating patterns, hinting at the molecule's double-helix shape.

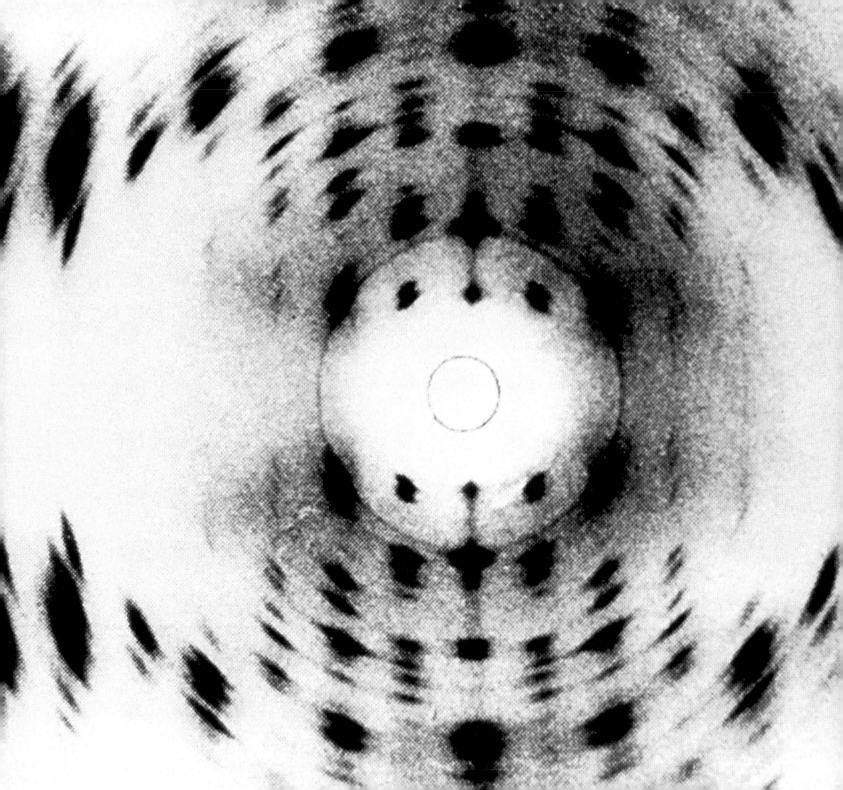

X RAY DIFFRACTION

X ray diffraction, developed in the early 1900s, is a way to analyze the structure of a molecule. First, a sample of the molecule is made into crystals with a repeating structure. When X rays are aimed through a crystal, they are bent, or diffracted. The direction in which they are bent depends on the locations of the atoms in the crystal sample. The final direction of the X rays can be recorded on film. Different structures scatter the X rays into different patterns. Physicist William Lawrence Bragg discovered a way to calculate the positions of the atoms within a crystal based on the X ray diffraction pattern. Bragg and his father, William Henry Bragg, won the Nobel Prize for Physics in 1915 for this work.

Compton Crick to collaborate with him. They began studying the structure of DNA, creating models of how it might look.

Meanwhile, Rosalind Franklin was at work on the same problem. Franklin was a brilliant chemist. In 1950, she had been invited to King's College London to join Wilkins at Randall's laboratory. However, Franklin and Wilkins had personality differences from the start and did not get along. Their poor relationship had a critical impact on the race to figure out the structure of DNA.

Instead of making models as did Watson and Crick, Franklin focused on improving the X ray diffraction photographs of DNA. She was a very careful scientist, and she wanted to publish her ideas only when she was absolutely sure of them.

In 1952, chemist Erwin Chargaff came to Cambridge University. He met with Watson and Crick, and he shared his data on the ratios of nucleotide bases in DNA. His work gave them new ideas on how the four nucleotide bases could fit together in DNA's structure.

Erwin CHARGAFF

Erwin Chargaff was an Austrian biochemist who immigrated to the United States after being forced to resign his position at the University of Berlin in 1933. At that time, the Nazi Party controlled Germany and enacted harsh restrictions against Jewish people, including scientists like Chargaff. In a series of innovative experiments performed at Columbia University in the 1940s, Chargaff showed that adenine and thymine always appeared in equal amounts in any given DNA molecule. The same was true for the nucleotide bases guanine and cytosine. His work gave Watson and Crick vital clues about how to match up the nucleotide bases in their double helix model.

PHOTO 51

Photo 51 was the critical piece of Franklin's data that Wilkins showed Watson. The X pattern on the X ray diffraction picture revealed the helical structure of DNA. Four white diamonds of empty space around the X shape indicated the helical structure continued below and above the picture, meaning the structure repeated. Spaces between the darker bands and lighter bands on the X shape helped Watson and Crick calculate distances between the different atoms that make up DNA. Large white spaces near the tips of the four arms of the X shape indicated that it was not a single helix, but a double helix. From this single image, the most important facts about DNA's structure could be calculated.

Early in 1953, Watson traveled to King's College London to suggest that he, Crick, Wilkins, and Franklin collaborate. Another researcher, Linus Pauling, had published a paper proposing the DNA structure was a triple helix, although he lacked data to support it. Watson spoke with Wilkins. In a fateful moment, Wilkins shared Franklin's latest X ray diffraction pictures with Watson. Franklin was not present, and the pictures were shared without her knowledge or consent. In fact, she was just weeks away from publishing her own research on the double helix structure.

With this key data in mind, Watson and Crick began constructing a double helix DNA model. Two strands of a phosphorous-rich backbone formed the sides. Pairs of nucleotide bases ran up the length of the molecule like rungs on a ladder. Adenine paired with thymine, and guanine paired with cytosine. The double helix structure made the molecule stable. Their proposed structure was published in a short article in *Nature* on April 25, 1953. In 1962, the Nobel Prize in Physiology or Medicine was awarded to Watson, Crick, and Wilkins. Franklin died in 1958, making

Watson, *left*, and Crick pose with a model demonstrating their proposed structure of DNA.

her ineligible to be nominated for the Nobel Prize. Watson admitted in 2003 that Franklin deserved to share the award.

Structure and Replication

Watson and Crick felt their proposed structure had major implications for DNA replication. They noted that since each nucleotide base could pair with only one other base, if one half of the strand was known, the other half would be known as well. They concluded this must be how the genetic messages of genes are copied prior to cell division. The DNA molecule would unzip to form two separate strands. Each separate strand would then serve as the template to make a new strand. In that way, one double helix would split and become two double helixes. This mode of replication is called semiconservative because part of the original molecule is conserved. One half of each new DNA molecule is old, and one half is new. This idea was proven correct in 1958 by Matthew Stanley Meselson and Franklin William Stahl.

Energized by the new knowledge, scientists launched into a new set of studies on DNA. They now knew that

By the mid 1950s, researchers had discovered that DNA replicated by splitting in half and joining with the corresponding nucleotide bases.

genes make enzymes, that genes are made of DNA, that DNA contains sequences of nucleotide bases, and that genes passed from parents' DNA to children's DNA. They even knew what molecules of DNA looked like. But how did the sequence of bases tell cells how to make enzymes? The answer was right around the corner.

Chapter Seven

Cracking the Code
OF LIFE

$$\frac{a+b}{a} = \frac{a}{b} = 1,618$$

A few years after Watson and Crick proposed the double helix structure of DNA, Crick put forth another landmark proposal. In 1957, Crick proposed two principles, neither of which was supported by direct experimental evidence at the time. The first he called the sequence hypothesis. This idea suggested that the order of nucleotide bases in a DNA strand represents a code for the amino acid sequence of a specific protein. Each set of bases in the code corresponds to a specific amino acid.

Crick's second proposed principle was one he called the "central dogma" of molecular biology.[1] This theory proposed that information in living systems goes from nucleic acids to proteins. Additionally, information in living systems cannot go the other way, from a protein to DNA or RNA. In other words, organisms can turn the coded information in genes into proteins, but they cannot turn the completed

Crick's principles of DNA paved the way for later genetic research.

proteins back into genetic code. Once Crick had outlined his ideas, many researchers began trying to understand the molecular machinery of the cell that allowed information to move from DNA to proteins.

Ribosomes, Transfer RNA, and Messenger RNA

Paul C. Zamecnik, a researcher at Harvard Medical School, used rat liver tissue to recreate a simple version of the interior of a cell in a test tube. After marking amino acids with radioactivity, he could track them as they were assembled into proteins. In 1956, Zamecnik was able to show that proteins are created on structures called ribosomes within cells.

A few years later, Zamecnik and his colleague Mahlon Hoagland discovered a special kind of RNA, the molecule that helps transport genetic instructions, that is needed for protein synthesis. Zamecnik and Hoagland noticed that some small RNA molecules became marked with the radioactive amino acids. Later, the RNA molecules transferred the marked amino acids to newly made proteins.

THE CENTRAL DOGMA

The word *dogma* means "a belief or set of beliefs that is accepted by the members of a group without being questioned or doubted."[2] Crick later admitted that naming his idea the central dogma was misleading. He wrote in his autobiography, "I had already used the obvious word hypothesis in the sequence hypothesis, and in addition I wanted to suggest that this new assumption was more central and more powerful. . . . As it turned out, the use of the word dogma caused almost more trouble than it was worth."[3]

From this the researchers concluded that the RNA molecules could act as an amino acid carrier. They called them transfer RNA, or tRNA. Zamecnik and Hoagland's idea was that the tRNA would transfer amino acids to the ribosome to add to the growing protein chain. Full details of their work were published in 1958.

Two years later, the three-man team of Matthew Stanley Meselson, François Jacob, and Sydney Brenner made another huge leap forward in understanding how genes code for proteins. Together they performed complicated experiments on the ribosomes of bacterial cells that had been infected with a virus. They found that an unstable type of long RNA was needed for the protein-building process. This RNA was different from the small RNA molecules Zamecnik and Hoagland had found. Meselson, Jacob, and Brenner called these longer RNA molecules messenger RNA, or mRNA.

The team proposed that strands of mRNA move through the structure of the ribosome. As a strand moves through, small pieces of tRNA, each carrying an amino acid, bind to the mRNA when they recognize the correct nucleotide bases.

THE AMAZING RIBOSOME

Ribosomes are necessary for cells to make proteins, and a single mammal cell can have as many as 10 million of them.[4] Mammals' bodies are made up largely of proteins, so a huge number must be produced to keep them alive. Ribosomes can link amino acids at a rate of 200 per minute.[5] At that rate, small proteins are made quickly. Two or three hours are needed for larger proteins. These include titin, a protein made up of 30,000 amino acids and which is an important component of muscles.[6]

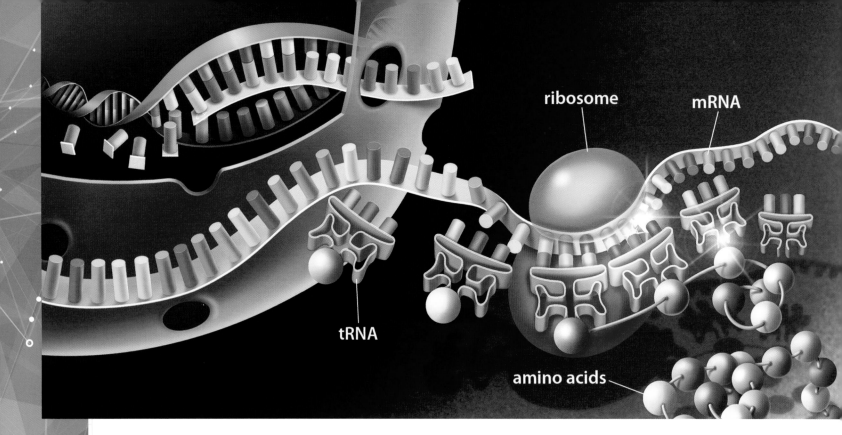

The ribosome assembles a long chain of amino acids using mRNA and tRNA, eventually forming a protein.

The amino acids then bond together chemically. In this way, a protein is made, amino acid by amino acid.

Cracking the Code

The next breakthrough in cracking the DNA code came from Marshall Nirenberg and J. Heinrich Matthaei, researchers at the National Institutes of Health in the United

States. On May 27, 1961, Matthaei did an experiment with a synthetic mRNA made only of uracil, a nucleotide base found in RNA but not DNA. In RNA, it takes the place of thymine. He found that a series of three uracil bases in a row (UUU) made only one kind of protein, made up of a chain of the amino acid phenylalanine. It was clear that UUU coded for phenylalanine. The first triplet code, now called a codon, was solved. Different sets of three bases would generate different amino acids.

There was still much work to be done to crack the rest of the code. By 1966, Nirenberg and other scientists had deciphered all 64 codons.[7] Nirenberg was awarded the Nobel Prize in Physiology or Medicine in 1968 for this work.

With the codons deciphered, scientists now sought to unlock the remaining secrets hidden within the genetic code. Much of genetics to this point had been a science of observation and of describing how things work. Now, scientists were poised not only to read but also to edit the codes that make up living things.

THE GENETIC CODE

How did Crick conclude the genetic code was made up of sequences of three nucleotide bases? If one nucleotide coded for one amino acid, DNA could only code for four different amino acids. If two nucleotides were used, there could only be 16 possible combinations, fewer than the number of known amino acids. A triplet combination would allow for 64 possible combinations. This suggested to researchers that more than one codon might correspond to each of the 20 common amino acids. This proved correct. Additionally, three codons are reserved for a "stop" function; rather than corresponding to an amino acid, they tell the ribosome a particular protein has been completed and should be released.

Editing the
WORDS OF LIFE

In the late 1950s, Swiss microbiologist Werner Arber studied viruses that infect bacteria, called bacteriophages. These can often be very infectious in one type of bacteria but die when they try to infect other types. Arber suggested some strains of bacteria might inactivate the viruses by cutting up the virus DNA with enzymes. He thought enzymes might recognize a specific sequence of nucleotide bases in viral DNA. Once bound to that special sequence, the enzymes could cut the DNA at that point. He called these restriction enzymes.

In 1970, American researcher Hamilton O. Smith and his colleagues at Johns Hopkins University purified an enzyme from the bacteria *Haemophilus influenzae* that seemed to fit Arber's idea. The enzyme recognized a short sequence of six DNA base pairs, or two codons, and cut it apart. Importantly, the enzyme, which Smith named

Arber's work with bacteriophages led to discoveries about enzymes that would open up a new field of genetics.

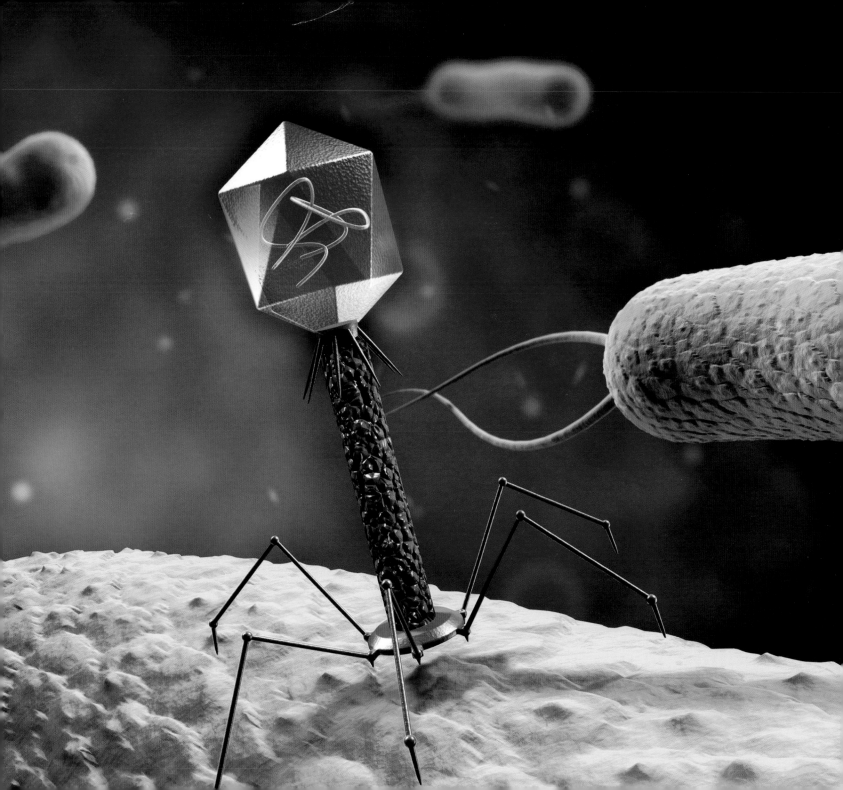

HindII, always cut at the same location in exactly the same way. Smith and Arber shared the Nobel Prize in Physiology or Medicine in 1978.

Cut, Paste, and Copy

Scientists quickly realized they could use restriction enzymes to cut DNA at specific places. Another discovery in 1967 showed they could also paste it back together. In that year, five different laboratories identified and purified an enzyme called DNA ligase from bacterial cells. DNA ligase can seal broken DNA strands back together.

The next big breakthrough started as scribbles on the back of a napkin at a scientific meeting in Hawaii. The meeting, held in November 1972, was about plasmids. Plasmids are tiny loops of DNA within bacterial cells. These loops are not part of the regular bacterial genome. Plasmids can contain useful genes, such as one that makes a bacterial cell resistant to an antibiotic. Plasmids can be passed between mature bacterial cells via small tubelike structures the bacteria create in their cell walls.

RESTRICTION ENZYMES

More than 800 different restriction enzymes have been purified from bacteria.[1] Each recognizes a particular restriction site. Most restriction sites are four to six bases long and are palindromic. That is, the sequence reads the same way forward and backward. The most useful enzymes make "sticky" cuts. These cuts are diagonal from each other and leave small single-strand DNA overhangs on each side. These "sticky ends" allow for easy pasting of DNA fragments together.

Plasmids exist and replicate independently of a cell's genome.

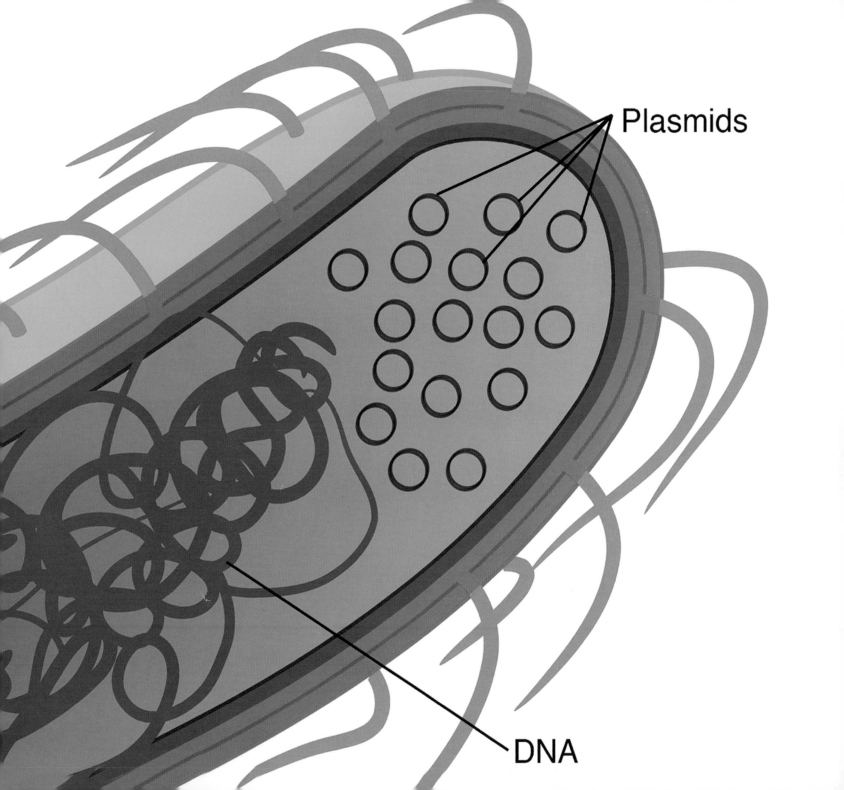

Plasmids

DNA

In 1971, researcher Stanley Cohen had figured out how to force bacterial cells to import plasmids that were floating free. Cohen attended the scientific meeting in Hawaii in 1972. There he met researcher Herbert Boyer of the University of California, San Francisco. Over dinner one night, the two scientists devised a scheme. They were going to use restriction enzymes, ligase, and plasmids to cut, paste, and copy DNA in a laboratory.

Boyer and Cohen's experiment used two plasmids. The first had a gene that would make an *E. coli* bacterial cell resistant to the antibiotic tetracycline. The second had a gene that would make the same kind of cell resistant to kanamycin, another antibiotic. The two plasmids were mixed in a test tube and then exposed to a restriction enzyme. The enzyme made cuts at a specific DNA sequence wherever the sequence occurred on the two plasmids. Ligase was added next to seal up the cuts. In a few instances, the antibiotic resistance genes from both plasmids pasted together. This created a new plasmid with both genes in it. Bacteria without resistance to the antibiotics were then added to the mixture of plasmids and forced to import them.

Cohen went on to win a Nobel Prize in Medicine in 1986.

BIOETHICS

Bioethics is the study of how ideas about fairness, respect, benefit, and harm should shape scientific research. When Boyer and Cohen made the first genetically modified organisms (GMOs), many were frightened. They feared recombinant DNA for a terrible gene, such as one that causes cancer, might escape a laboratory in a common bacteria and infect people around the world. In 1973, the US government created a committee to study recombinant DNA technology. Notable research scientists published letters in the journals *Science* and *Nature* asking researchers to temporarily halt recombinant DNA experiments. In 1975, a conference of scientists, lawyers, and other officials proposed safeguards to contain recombinant DNA work. This conference marked the dawn of modern bioethics.

The bacteria were then separated and grown in petri dishes containing tetracycline and kanamycin. Only the bacterial cells that had taken up the new plasmid containing both protective genes survived. For the very first time, human beings had cut and pasted genes in a laboratory by combining genes from two plasmids. What's more, the genes did what they were supposed to do. They made proteins that allowed the cells to survive two different antibiotics.

Boyer and Cohen published their data in early 1973. Afterward, some scientists wondered if the technique would only work with plasmids from bacteria. Boyer and Cohen performed another experiment showing it did not matter which type of organism the DNA came from. Frog DNA was cut and pasted into plasmids, and then bacterial cells were forced to take up those new plasmids. When the bacteria were grown in test tubes in the laboratory, they made frog proteins. The new technology was called recombinant DNA, because it combined DNA from more than one source.

Now scientists had new power to cut, paste, and copy DNA. But their inability to easily read the nucleotide base pair sequences of DNA became a major block to further discovery. Progress was made in 1977, when American scientist Walter Gilbert and English scientist Frederick Sanger independently developed new techniques for rapid DNA sequencing. Their techniques could quickly sequence 900 bases at a time.[2] For this work, Gilbert and Sanger shared the Nobel Prize in Chemistry in 1980.

Moving DNA

The ability to sequence DNA and to cut and paste it in the laboratory opened many doors for genetics research. In the late 1970s, Yale University researcher Frank Ruddle became interested in using mice to study human genetic diseases. Along with fellow scientist Jon W. Gordon, he decided to produce the first transgenic animal, or organism containing a gene or genes from another species or breed of organism. He reasoned he could study human genes in mice since mice and humans share many genes in common.

Because of ethical concerns about human DNA experimentation, Ruddle and Gordon started with viral DNA. First, they used recombinant DNA techniques to make a fragment of DNA containing genes from two viruses. Using a glass tube finer than a human hair, they injected the fragment into newly fertilized mouse eggs. The eggs were then transferred into female mice. After the baby mice were born, they were tested for viral DNA. Out of 78 mice, two tested positive.[3] When those mice matured, they were mated to normal mice. The viral genes were passed to some of their offspring. These results were published in 1981 in the journal *Science*.

Building on this work, researchers Mario R. Capecchi from the University of Utah, Martin Evans from Cardiff University in the United Kingdom, and Oliver Smithies from the University of North Carolina at Chapel Hill created the first knockout mouse in 1989. A knockout mouse is one in which a normal gene has been precisely replaced with a broken, mutated copy. This "knocks out" the ability of that gene to make its protein. In this way, scientists can figure out what genes of unknown function might do in the body. The three were awarded the Nobel Prize in Physiology or Medicine in 2007 for their work.

Soon a new field was born: genetic engineering. Genetic engineering is the science of altering the DNA of a cell. It is used for research and for making protein drugs in laboratories. Genetic engineering is also concerned with correcting genetic defects and with making improvements to plants and animals bred by humans. Humans have been practicing a simple form of genetic engineering for thousands of years, selectively breeding crops such as corn to have desired traits. This field of science has become much more powerful in the last few decades. Since 1989, researchers have increasingly used genetic engineering to study gene functions and cure disease.

By the 2010s, important crops such as corn were genetically engineered to resist herbicides and insects.

Making a Knockout Mouse

1. A DNA fragment with a broken copy of a gene of interest is made.

2. Stem cells from a black-haired mouse embryo are forced to import the fragment. In a small number of cells, the normal gene is successfully swapped out of the genome, and the broken gene is swapped in.

3. The embryonic stem cells that have successfully swapped genes are injected into growing embryos from a white-haired mouse.

4. The embryos are transferred to a surrogate mother mouse. The injected embryos now have two kinds of cells. Some cells have a normal gene of interest and a white coat color gene. Some cells have the broken gene of interest and a black coat color gene. They have white-and-black spotted coats.

5. The spotted mice are mated to normal white mice. In some cases, the germ cells from a spotted mouse will have the broken gene of interest and black coat color gene. If so, the resulting offspring will have fully black-haired coats. These black mice will have one copy of the broken gene of interest from the spotted parent and one copy of the normal gene of interest from the white-haired parent.

6. The black mice offspring are mated together. One-quarter of them will have two broken copies of the gene of interest. Any differences in the behavior, appearance, or other characteristics of these mice are likely linked to the gene of interest.

The mouse at left had a gene linked to obesity removed. The mouse at right did not have the gene removed.

The Future of
GENETICS

The details of how genes function are still a major part of genetics research. However, with the creation of the first transgenic animals, genetics has became more and more a science of intervention and invention rather than simple discovery. The sequence of nearly the entire human genome was completed in 2003. With that information in hand, many new genetic engineering technologies and areas of study have emerged.

Making Proteins to
Treat Human Disease

Since the 1980s, proteins made in the laboratory using recombinant DNA technology have emerged as a major new class of medicines. Usually these are produced by inserting human genes into bacterial cells or yeast cells. The transgenic bacteria or

$$\frac{a+b}{a} = \frac{a}{b} = 1.618$$

Once DNA's structure and function were understood, researchers studied new ways to manipulate it.

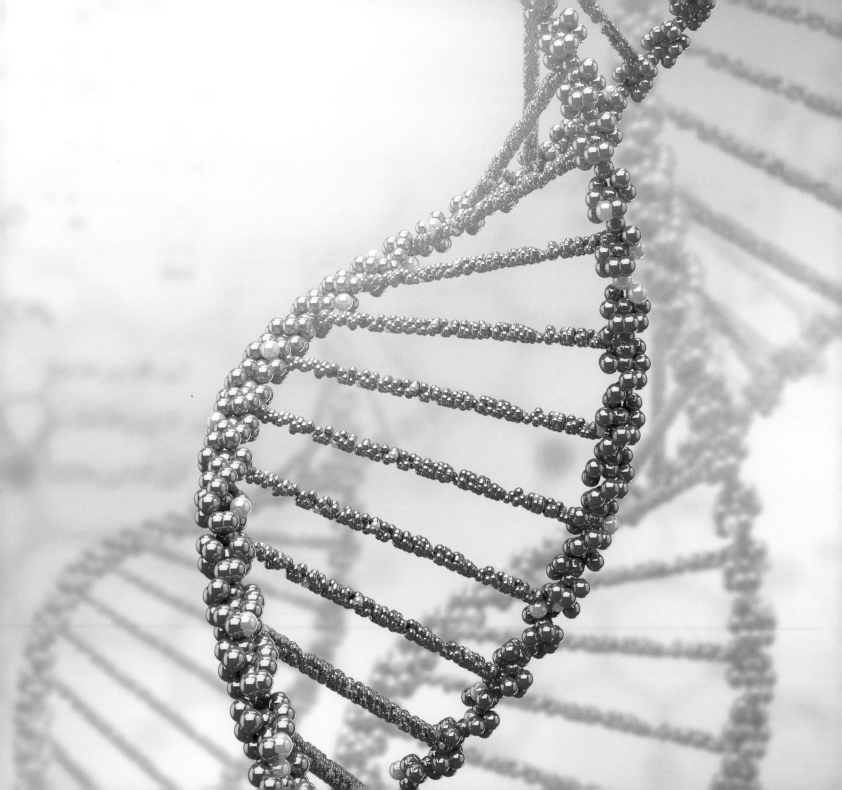

yeasts are grown in very large cultures and produce large quantities of the desired protein. The first recombinant human protein medicine was insulin, which is used to treat diabetes.

Protein medicines can be used to replace a protein that is lacking or abnormal in a patient. They can also be used to interfere with a disease process. An example of this type of medicine is a protein that binds to a cancer cell and causes it to die. Today there are more than 200 approved recombinant protein medicines in the United States.[1] Many more are in development.

Cloning

Clones are organisms that are, like identical twins, exact genetic copies of another organism. The most famous is Dolly the sheep, born in 1996. She was cloned from a cell taken from the udder of a six-year-old female sheep.

There are two types of cloning: reproductive and therapeutic. In reproductive cloning, scientists create an embryo genetically identical to an adult donor animal.

INSULIN

Before the discovery of insulin, diabetes was a fatal disease with no cure. In 1922, human tests revealed natural insulin, extracted from the cow pancreas and purified, could help patients with diabetes live longer, healthier lives. Arthur Riggs and Keiichi Itakura of the Beckman Research Institute of the City of Hope, in collaboration with Herbert Boyer of the company Genentech, produced the first genetically engineered recombinant insulin using *E. coli* in 1978. Genentech began to sell the insulin in 1982. Today, the vast majority of insulin used to treat diabetes worldwide is a recombinant protein.

In the late 1990s, Dolly became a symbol of the new science of mammal cloning.

Spotlight on Cloning

Both therapeutic and reproductive cloning rely on a technology called somatic cell nuclear transfer.

1. The nucleus is carefully removed from a cell of an adult donor animal.

2. The nucleus is carefully removed from an egg cell of the same species of animal.

3. The donor nucleus is injected into the egg.

4. The resulting embryo is prompted to start dividing using electrical pulses or certain chemicals.

5. The embryo is allowed to grow in a petri dish.

At this point, the two techniques differ. In therapeutic cloning, embryonic stem cells are taken from the cloned embryo. In reproductive cloning, the growing embryo is transferred to the uterus of a surrogate mother, where it may develop into a fetus. When it is born, the resulting animal is a clone of the donor animal.

The process of reproductive cloning is very difficult. When researchers in 1996 cloned Dolly, a total of 277 cell fusions were made. Of these, only 29 early embryos developed. These were transferred into 13 surrogate mothers.[2] Only one pregnancy ended in a healthy birth.

By 2014, scientists were cloning dozens of cows each year.

This embryo is transferred to the uterus of a surrogate mother, and a cloned animal is born. In therapeutic cloning, an embryo is created in a similar way, but the resulting cells are grown in a laboratory. They are not transferred into a female animal's uterus.

Scientists have successfully used reproductive cloning to produce mice, cattle, goats, pigs, deer, rabbits, cats, mules, and horses. No cloning of human beings for reproductive purposes has been done. Many countries have banned human reproductive cloning, although many states in the United States do not have specific laws against it. Currently, there are no federal laws banning cloning in the United States.

Therapeutic cloning can be used to make stem cells. These cells are capable of developing into any other type of body cell, including those found in muscles, organs, and the brain. The potential for using stem cells to repair organs makes them a major area of research. In 2013, Shoukhrat Mitalipov of Oregon Health & Science University, along with his colleagues, reported in the journal *Cell* that they successfully used therapeutic cloning to grow human stem cells in a petri dish. Research is under way to determine how such cells might be used to treat human disease.

Gene Therapy

Gene therapy may allow doctors to treat a disease by inserting specific genes into a patient's genome. There are three current approaches under investigation. One is to replace a mutated gene that causes a human disease with a healthy copy of the gene.

Gene therapy drugs require expensive equipment and techniques to produce, making them among the costliest drugs.

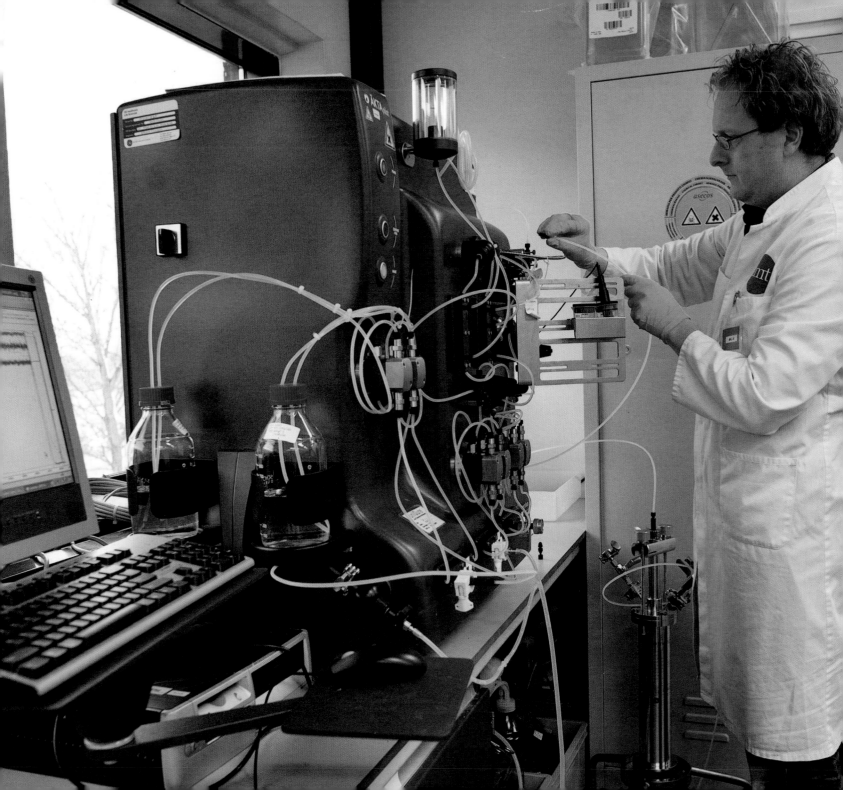

Another is to inactivate, or knock out, a mutated gene that is not working properly. A third is to insert an entirely new gene into the genome to help fight a disease.

Despite the promise of gene therapy, however, the techniques involved are still risky. Serious health issues can occur, including cancer. Gene therapy is currently being tested only for the treatment of diseases that have no other cures, such as the bleeding disorder hemophilia. It is hoped that better techniques in the future may allow gene therapy to be widely used to treat many human diseases.

Mapping the Human Proteome

Unlike the genome, the types of protein present in a cell or organism change constantly. The word *proteome* has been coined to describe the group of proteins existing in a particular sample at a particular time. Many diseases involve defective proteins in the body. Therefore, the study of the proteome will likely play an important future role in drug discovery and the diagnosis and treatment of disease.

Several researchers have made efforts to catalog all of the proteins contained in the human proteome. Among them are Akhilesh Pandey of Johns Hopkins University in Maryland and Bernhard Küster of the Technical University of Munich in Germany. In May 2014, both researchers posted rough drafts of a Human Proteome Map online and published an article on the subject in the journal *Nature*.

Some gene therapies involve growing specialized viruses to deliver the corrected gene to cells.

Beyond the DNA Code

Control of some genetic traits can be influenced by factors outside of an organism's DNA sequence. The study of these factors is called epigenetics. Epigenetic changes happen when outside factors attach certain molecules to DNA or to the proteins that DNA winds around to make chromosomes. The sequence of the DNA stays the same. Yet the epigenetic changes can switch genes on or off and determine which genes produce proteins.

Epigenetic changes are a normal part of development in many cases. An individual's cells all contain the complete set of his or her DNA, but the body contains many different types of cells. Cell types differ because they have certain sets of genes that are expressed, or turned on, as well as other sets that are not expressed, or turned off. But epigenetic changes can also be responsible for some diseases. Improper epigenetic changes have been associated with cancer, diseases involving the chromosomes, and intellectual disabilities.

Genetic research makes it possible to link diseases with specific genes. This may lead to precisely targeted genetic therapies.

HOW TO MAP A PROTEOME

For the proteome mapping research, both teams analyzed human tissue samples. Samples were exposed to enzymes that break proteins into shorter chunks. Specialized devices that read the amino acid sequence of proteins then analyzed these chunks. Pandey's team generated data from healthy human tissues. The approach of Küster's group was to first compile existing data from databases and colleagues. To fill in gaps, the Küster group then analyzed human tissues, body fluids, and cancer cells.

Epigenetic treatments are in development. These drugs are aimed at reversing the epigenetic changes causing improper gene silencing. However, as with gene therapy, scientists and doctors are proceeding very carefully. Epigenetic processes and changes are widespread in normal cells, and they differ in different types of cells. To be successful, epigenetic treatments must affect only the abnormal cells that need to be changed.

The Future of Genetics

From pea plants to proteomes, the field of genetics has come incredibly far in just 150 years. The future of genetics will likely focus heavily on predicting, treating, and curing human diseases known to be caused by genetic and epigenetic changes. Eventually, the genetics of complex diseases such as heart disease or cancer will become much more clear. This should help researchers create more effective medical treatments with fewer side effects.

Many new initiatives have been launched to support this goal. For example, the Cancer Genome Atlas project is trying to identify all the genetic abnormalities seen in 50 major types of cancer. Similarly, Autism Speaks, an organization that funds and promotes autism research, is partnering with Google to put the complete genome sequences from 10,000 autism patients online for researchers to use in their studies.[3] Thanks to a series of brilliant and innovative scientists and experience spanning more than a century, humanity has cracked the code that makes us who we are.

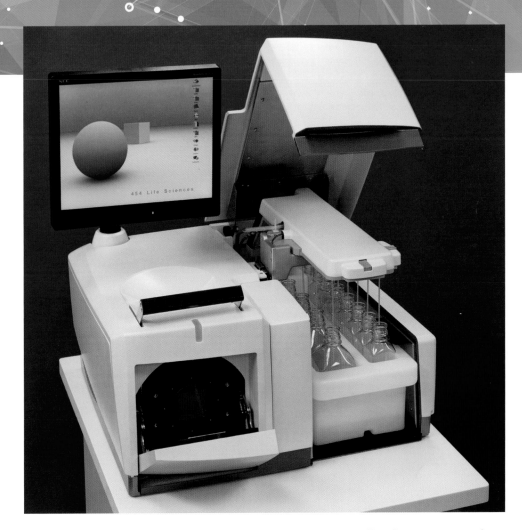

Smaller, faster, and cheaper genome sequencing machines will make it easier to take patients' genetics into account.

Timeline

1866 Gregor Mendel publishes his results regarding his three laws of heredity. He distributes copies of his papers but is ignored.

1879 Walther Flemming discovers chromosomes but does not understand their true significance.

1900 Hugo de Vries, Erich von Tschermak, and Carl Correns independently rediscover Mendel's three laws.

1902 Walter Sutton and Theodor Boveri develop the chromosome theory of inheritance.

1905 Nettie Stevens publishes her data supporting the XY model of sex determination.

1910 Thomas Hunt Morgan discovers sex-linked traits while studying fruit flies.

1941 George Beadle and Edward Tatum, working with the mold *Neurospora*, propose the "one gene, one enzyme" theory.

1944 Oswald Theodore Avery publishes evidence that DNA in chromosomes, rather than proteins, is the hereditary material.

1953 James Watson and Francis Crick propose the three-dimensional double helix structure of DNA.

1957 Crick proposes the sequence hypothesis and the central dogma of molecular biology.

1960 Matthew Meselson, François Jacob, and Sydney Brenner discover messenger RNA.

1961 Marshall Nirenberg and J. Heinrich Matthaei identify a codon in mRNA, UUU, which codes for the amino acid phenylalanine.

1970 Hamilton O. Smith discovers restriction enzymes from bacteria that can be used to cut DNA at precise sequences.

1973 Herbert Boyer and Stanley N. Cohen develop recombinant DNA and make bacterial cells that can produce frog proteins.

1977 Walter Gilbert and Frederick Sanger invent two different methods for the rapid sequencing of DNA.

1981 Frank Ruddle and Jon Gordon create the first transgenic mouse.

1996 Researchers successfully clone a large mammal for the first time, a sheep named Dolly.

2003 The first full draft of the human genome sequence is completed.

2014 Akhilesh Pandey and Bernhard Küster publish the first maps of the human proteome.

Essential Facts

Genetic Mapping

This is a way to determine the order of genes on a chromosome. The closer together two genes are, the less likely a crossover will take place between them during meiosis. Thomas Hunt Morgan first proposed genetic mapping in 1911. It was his student, Alfred Sturtevant, who actually accomplished most of the mapping of the fruit fly chromosomes.

X ray Diffraction

Developed in the early 1900s, this is a way to analyze the structure of a molecule. The molecule of interest is formed into a crystal. The crystal is bombarded with X rays, and the resulting "bent" X rays are captured on film. James Watson and Francis Crick used X ray diffraction images, some of them captured by Rosalind Franklin, to determine the double helix structure of DNA.

DNA Sequencing

To sequence a strand of DNA is to determine the ordered list of nucleotide bases that make up the strand. Two different sequencing techniques were invented in 1977 by Walter Gilbert and Frederick Sanger. Their techniques could quickly sequence up to 900 bases at a time. In 1992, a quicker but less accurate method called "shotgun sequencing" was developed by J. Craig Venter.

IMPACT ON SCIENCE

The science of genetics has solved a mystery human beings have struggled with for millennia: how do parents pass on traits to their children? Deciphering the genetic code has enhanced our understanding of ourselves and of all other species. It has also yielded practical benefits. Scientists can now develop specialized medical treatments that reach all the way down to the basic building blocks of our bodies. As these techniques advance, diseases linked to our genes may become things of the past.

KEY ORGANISMS IN GENETICS

Many discoveries in genetics were made possible by experimenting with organisms well suited to scientists' experiments. The distinct features of Mendel's pea plants made it easy to calculate the ratios of different traits between generations. Scientists in the late 1800s used sea urchin cells to study fertilization because it was easy to see through the transparent cells into the inner workings of the cellular processes. The inexpensive and quickly reproducing fruit fly gave Thomas Hunt Morgan an ideal animal with which to study sex-linked characteristics. Knockout mice continue to be used today to investigate gene functions.

QUOTE

"We are here to celebrate the completion of the first survey of the entire human genome. Without a doubt, this is the most important, most wondrous map ever produced. . . . More than 1,000 researchers across six nations have revealed nearly all 3 billion letters of our miraculous genetic code."

—President Bill Clinton at the press conference to announce the completion of the first draft of the human genome sequence, June 26, 2000

Glossary

amino acid

A basic molecular building block of a protein.

botany

The study of plants.

chromosome

A tightly packed combination of DNA and proteins located in the nucleus of a cell.

clone

An organism that is an exact genetic copy of another organism.

cytologist

A scientist who studies cells.

deoxyribonucleic acid (DNA)

A molecule that encodes the genetic instructions used in the development and functioning of all living organisms. It is tightly wound together with proteins to form chromosomes.

enzyme

A protein that facilitates a biochemical reaction.

epigenetics

The study of heritable changes in gene activity that are not caused by changes in the DNA sequence.

gene

A physical unit of heredity.

genetics

The science of heredity.

genome

The entire set of genetic information contained on the chromosomes of an organism.

heredity

The passage of biological traits from parents to offspring.

medium

A substance on which an organism lives and grows.

mutation

A change in the normal DNA sequence of a gene.

nucleotide base

Any one of the four molecules present in DNA that make up the genetic sequence.

plasmid

A small section of DNA in bacteria that is separate from their genome.

proteome

All of the proteins present in one sample of a cell, tissue, or organism at a certain point in time.

recombinant DNA

Using laboratory techniques to cut and paste DNA from two different species or breeds of organism together.

recombinant protein

A protein produced in the laboratory using recombinant DNA technology. Recombinant proteins are often used as medicines to treat diseases.

sequence

The order of nucleotide bases in a segment of DNA.

trait

A characteristic of an organism that can be passed to offspring.

Additional Resources

Selected Bibliography

Pierce, Benjamin A. *Genetics Essentials: Concepts and Connections*. New York: W. H. Freeman, 2013. Print.

Schwartz, James. *In Pursuit of the Gene: From Darwin to DNA*. Cambridge, MA: Harvard UP, 2008. Print.

Watson, James D., and Andrew Berry. *DNA: The Secret of Life*. New York: Knopf, 2003. Print.

Further Readings

Carmichael, L. E. *Gene Therapy*. Minneapolis, MN: Abdo, 2014. Print.

Hodge, Russ. *Genetic Engineering: Manipulating the Mechanisms of Life*. New York: Facts on File, 2009. Print.

Mooney, Carla, and Samuel Carbaugh. *Genetics: Breaking the Code of Your DNA*. White River Junction, Vermont: Nomad, 2014. Print.

Simpson, Kathleen, and Sarah Tishkoff. *Genetics: From DNA to Designer Dogs*. Washington, DC: National Geographic, 2008. Print.

Websites

To learn more about History of Science, visit **booklinks.abdopublishing.com**. These links are routinely monitored and updated to provide the most current information available.

For More Information

J. Craig Venter Institute
9704 Medical Center Drive
Rockville, MD 20850
301-795-7000

http://www.jcvi.org
The J. Craig Venter Institute, founded by one of the major researchers of the Human Genome Project, conducts research focusing on the genome. It also engages in education projects, teaching students about genomics and other sciences.

National Human Genome Research Institute
National Institutes of Health
Building 31, Room 4B09
31 Center Drive, MSC 2152
9000 Rockville Pike
Bethesda, MD 20892
301-402-0911

http://www.genome.gov
The National Human Genome Research Institute was established in the 1980s to participate in the Human Genome Project. Today, it operates as a research institute under the umbrella of the National Institutes of Health, studying the relationship between genetics and diseases.

Source Notes

Chapter 1. The Human Genome Project

1. "President Clinton, British Prime Minister Tony Blair Deliver Remarks on Human Genome Milestone." *CNN Transcripts*. CNN, 26 June 2000. Web. 14 Sept. 2014.

2. Nicholas Wade. "Scientists Complete Rough Draft of Human Genome." *New York Times*. New York Times, 26 June 2000. Web. 14 Sept. 2014.

3. "The Human Genome Project Completion: Frequently Asked Questions." *Newsroom*. National Human Genome Research Institute, 30 Oct. 2010. Web. 14 Sept. 2014.

4. Anne Buboltz. "Pages from the First Human Genome." *Broad Institute*. Broad Institute, 18 Oct. 2010. Web. 14 Sept. 2014.

5. Renato Dulbecco. "A Turning Point in Cancer Research: Sequencing the Human Genome." *Science* 231.4742 (1986): 1055–1056. Print.

6. "Human Genome Project Budget." *Human Genome Project Information Archive*. Oak Ridge National Laboratory, 23 July 2013. Web. 14 Sept. 2014.

7. "The Human Genome Project Completion: Frequently Asked Questions." *Newsroom*. National Human Genome Research Institute, 30 Oct. 2010. Web. 14 Sept. 2014.

8. "The Human Genome Project." *Essential Biochemistry Instructor Resources*. Wiley, 2004. Web. 14 Sept. 2014.

9. "The Human Genome Project Completion: Frequently Asked Questions." *Newsroom*. National Human Genome Research Institute, 30 Oct. 2010. Web. 14 Sept. 2014.

10. "How Much Did the Apollo Program Cost?" *Curiosity.com*. Discovery Channel, 2011. Web. 15 Sept. 2014.

11. Brad Plumer. "NASA Wants to Keep the International Space Station Going until 2024." *Wonkblog*. Washington Post, 9 Jan. 2014. Web. 15 Sept. 2014.

12. Alex Knapp. "How Much Does it Cost to Find a Higgs Boson?" *Forbes*. Forbes, 5 July 2012. Web. 15 Sept. 2014.

13. "The Human Genome Project." *Stanford Encyclopedia of Philosophy*. Stanford University, 26 Nov. 2008. Web. 14 Sept. 2014.

14. "Celera Genomics Publishes First Analysis of Human Genome." *Celera*. Celera, 12 Feb. 2001. Web. 14 Sept. 2014.

Chapter 2. A Gardener Discovers Genes

None.

Chapter 3. Making Sense of Mendel

None.

Chapter 4. Mapping Genes to Chromosomes

1. Victoria Sherrow. "Morgan, Thomas Hunt." *Great Scientists*. Facts on File, 1992. Web. 15 Sept. 2014.

2. James Schwartz. *In Pursuit of the Gene: From Darwin to DNA*. Cambridge, MA: Harvard UP, 2008. Print. 180.

3. T. H. Morgan. "The Scientific Work of Miss N. M. Stevens." *Science* 36.928 (1912): 468-470. Print.

4. "The Nobel Prize in Physiology or Medicine 1933." *Nobelprize.org*. Nobel Media, 2014. Web. 15 Sept. 2014.

5. "Award Ceremony Speech: Nobel Prize in Physiology or Medicine 1933." *Nobelprice.org*. Nobel Media, 2014. Web. 15 Sept. 2014.

Chapter 5. Genes, Proteins, and DNA

1. James Schwartz. *In Pursuit of the Gene: From Darwin to DNA*. Cambridge, MA: Harvard UP, 2008. Print. 240.

2. Paul Berg. *George Beadle: An Uncommon Farmer*. Cold Spring Harbor, NY: Cold Spring Harbor Laboratory P, 2003. Print. 143.

3. Ibid. 145.

4. James D. Watson and Andrew Berry. *DNA: The Secret of Life*. New York: Knopf, 2003. Print. 40.

Chapter 6. The Double Helix

None.

$$\frac{a+b}{a} = \frac{a}{b} = 1{,}618$$

Source Notes Continued

Chapter 7. Cracking the Code of Life

1. "The Francis Crick Papers." *Profiles in Science*. National Laboratory of Medicine, n.d. Web. 15 Sept. 2014.

2. "Dogma." *Merriam-Webster*. Merriam-Webster, 2014. Web. 14 Sept. 2014.

3. Francis Crick. *What Mad Pursuit: A Personal View of Scientific Discovery*. New York: Basic, 1988. Print. 109.

4. "Ribosome." *British Society of Cell Biology*. British Society for Cell Biology, n.d. Web. 14 Sept. 2014.

5. Ibid.

6. Ibid.

7. "The Marshall W. Nirenberg Papers." *Profiles in Science*. National Laboratory of Medicine, n.d. Web. 15 Sept. 2014.

Chapter 8. Editing the Words of Life

1. Leslie A. Pray. "Restriction Enzymes." *Nature Education*. Nature Education, 2008. Web. 15 Sept. 2014.

2. "Sanger Sequencing." *Centre for Applied Neurogenetics*. Center for Applied Neurogenetics, 2014. Web. 15 Sept. 2014.

3. Dennis Jones. "Genetic Engineering of a Mouse." *Yale Journal of Biology and Medicine*. Yale Journal of Biology and Medicine, 2011. Web. 15 Sept. 2014.

$$\frac{a+b}{a} = \frac{a}{b} = 1.618$$

Chapter 9. The Future of Genetics

1. Paul J. Carter. "Introduction to Current and Future Protein Therapeutics: A Protein Engineering Perspective." *Experimental Cell Research* 317.9 (2011): 1261–1269. Print.

2. "Animal Cloning." *Understanding Animal Research*. Understanding Animal Research, 2014. Web. 15 Sept. 2015.

3. Devin Coldewey. "Massive Autism Database Finds Home on Google's Cloud." *NBC News*. NBC News, 9 June 2014. Web. 15 Sept. 2014.

$$\frac{a+b}{a} = \frac{a}{b} = 1.618$$

Index

About the Author

Jillian Lokere is a science and medical writer who specializes in communicating complex scientific information in an engaging and approachable way. She has a BS in Biological Sciences from Stanford University and an MS in Genetics from Harvard University. She lives north of Boston, Massachusetts, with her husband and three children.